WISE GIRL

How the Mafia Taught Me to Succeed on Wall Street... and in Comedy

BY
ELYSE DELUCCI

Disclaimer: I can't believe you're reading the fine print, but here we are. And that's a rule worth knowing: Always read the fine print, because usually, this is where it gets fugazi. Not here – obviously. This book is a work of nonfiction. The experiences, memories and words are the authors alone – And are true as I remember them, but lets be serious, sometimes memories can be hazy. Most of the names in this book have been changed to protect people's privacy.

Copyright © 2023 by Elyse DeLucci

First Edition

All rights reserved. No part of this book may be reproduced in any form or by any electronic or mechanical means, including information storage and retrieval systems, without permission in writing from the publisher, except a reviewer, who may quote brief passages in in a review. Scanning, uploading, and electronic distribution of this book or facilitation of such without the permission of the publisher is prohibited.

ISBN: 979-8-9867871-1-4

Printed in the United States

DEDICATION

This book is dedicated to naysayers, dream killers, and anyone who fired me.
No, seriously...

- To my daughters, precious treasures, Annalise and Vivienne, thank you for showing me what true love is.
- To Pauly the Tooth, for without you, none of this would be possible. I love you forever.
- To My Family, especially my Nonni, without you I'd have no material!
- To my Father, I wish you were alive to read this.
- To Chris, my partner, coffee maker and driver. I love you more everyday.

This book is dedicated to everyone who has the chutzpah to dream and make it a reality.

Now enough already, I'm making myself nauseous.

Praise for *Wise Girl*

"Couldn't put it down."

-Vincent Pastore, *The Sopranos*

"Elyse Delucci's WISE GIRL is truly funny. The only thing better than reading it, would be having a beer with her while she tells you her stories. If the Mafia taught her about comedy, I want to take that class!"

-Dennis Dugan, Director
*Happy Gilmore, Big Daddy,
I Now Pronounce You Chuck & Larry*

"I want to thank Elyse DeLucci for breaking the code of silence (Omertà #24) to write this book. She shares her totally relatable triumphs, failures, fears, anxieties and the wisdom that came from them. *Wise Girl* is a funny, heartfelt, field guide for seeing life as a journey and not a sentence."

-Adam Ferrara, Actor/Comedian

"Brutally honest, engaging and funny. What more could you want in a book?"

- Judy Gold, Comedian

"Reading "Wise Girl" I thought of the Charlie Parker song 'Bloomdido.' Elyse plays Jazz with her insightful stories. She exposes the ups and downs of her life, then manages to bring it all together with her style of humor. Served like we Italians love our pasta 'Al Dente' baby!"

Robert Funaro, *The Sopranos*

WISE GIRL

How the Mafia Taught Me to Succeed on Wall Street... and in Comedy

BURNABY

The only true wisdom is in knowing you know nothing.
— Socrates

You have power over your mind — not outside events. Realize this, and you will find strength.
— Marcus Aurelius

If anyone tries to stop you from doing it, do it anyway."
—Elyse DeLucci

TABLE OF CONTENTS

Introduction: A Woman in Business	1
The Rules List	9
Murder? Panic? Heartbreak?	12
Saying Goodbye	31
God, It Was Stuffy in There	52
The Italian-American Diaspora	67
Lemons to Limoncello	74
Interview in the Boiler Room	80
Why So Many Rules?	84
No One is Paying You to Gossip	88
Money Talks…Loud	91
Hobbies and Hustles	98

Cover Your Tush…	113
and Get Your Hand Off Mine	
Work Hazing	119
They Would Not Murder Each Other	123
And Introducing Elyse	132
Bosses Have Opinions	140
Respect the Commission	144
Two Steps Ahead	149
A Performer is Born	155
Omertà: The Code of Silence	165
Sprezzatura:	172
The Italian Art of Looking Great	
Keep Your Eyes Open	183
and You'll Find Versailles	
Nightgowns and Screaming	189
Reputation is Everything	194

Slice the Garlic Thin	199
So I Tried Stand-Up	202
If I Don't Do It, I'll Regret It	207
A Few Words on Mental Health	224
The Best Job I Ever Had	228
Sign off From Love Bunny Cottage	233
Glossary	235

Introduction:
A Woman Made in Business or
A Made Woman In Business?

Formal introductions are so awkward, don't you think? But I guess they're necessary because we probably don't know each other. Or, maybe we do? Maybe we've worked together in business, maybe you know me from the stage, or from your pocket as a social media and podcasting raconteur.

Regardless, my name is Elyse - fabulous to meet you. To give you a quick download: I'm a born and bred New Yorker, schlepped/begged/worked my ass off, and managed to have an executive level corporate career in publishing and on Wall Street (badass I'll admit) and now I'm a stand-up comedian (we'll get to that later).

But, this book? This book is about my corporate career and, no, I'm not going to bore you to tears, or worse - lecture you. I'm just going to tell you how I got there and the rules I learned growing up from my wild, enthusiastic and paranoid Italian-American family.

And yes, I've completed Executive Education programs at both Harvard Business School and Wharton - but that's not where I mastered the rules to the game. *School? It's for the birds.*

The rules I'm talking about I learned from home, as a little kid growing up in the greatest city in the world, surrounded by the colorful characters of my lovely-but-loud-and-sometime-scary *La Famiglia*. These helped me get (okay, strong arm) myself the jobs I wanted, as well as navigate the business world. To be honest, I might've not always followed them, but I learned them. The thing about the rules is that they have a peculiar way of repeating themselves until you pay attention.

What I want to share with you is what I learned, albeit scrappily, from one male-dominated world, and how to use it in order to succeed in another. Capisce? And to be clear, this book is not one of great intellect, most of the time, I walk around with not one intellectual thought in my head. *I do and dream and then do some more.*

Corporate executive and current stand-up comedian are two things that are not normally in a sentence together. I'm also the ex-wife of a charming British man, the mother of two small human beings. And we all live in harmony (*on good days*) in the glittery, fantasy-fueled, feral island of Manhattan.

Some people do better when they get a visual or see someone in their natural habitat – I know I do. Since you're reading this and we're not together in my living room, let me paint a picture for you. No, wait, let's turn up the music first: In background, I have on my daily jazz morning compilation: Harry James, "I've heard that song before" .. after this... "ZING! Went the strings of my heart", the version by Vince Giordano And The Nighthawks, then maybe "Take Me Back To Manhattan" by Rosemary Clooney...".C'est Si Bon" by Eartha Kitt..."They Can't Take That Away From Me" by Mel Torme... and now for the picture...

Right now, I'm typing in my pre-war apartment off 5th avenue in Manhattan's Upper East Side, which I bought after a search that lasted roughly 38 years. If you're counting, I've been looking for an apartment since I was in the womb. Like any decent Italian woman, I found this one like I've found my best wardrobe pieces: on sale, ragged in a discount store – where the masses are *never* looking. And that right there is a rule worth knowing.

My husband and I spent two years renovating and restoring my dream home to its pre-war glory. I'm traditional; I like ornate crown moldings but not in an eggshell color sense, so I chose to give our abode the old world glamorous Manhattan touch it deserved: Black and white checkerboard porcelain tile floors, gilded crystal chandeliers, warm terracotta walls, brass lamp-shaded wall sconces, leopard wall-to-wall carpeting, thick gold leaf frames and shadow boxes for every family photo and international treasure on display. Heaven.

I should tell you that I absolutely love being surrounded by luxurious interiors because I have a paralyzing ruinous fear of being poor. Growing up, I saw my parents struggle and I couldn't bear that for my own family. Let me be clear, I'll never own a monstrosity of a house; I don't like the idea of rattling around and hearing the echoes of voices. I love apartments because, usually, there's only one point of entry. What I'm saying is if I could shrink Versailles to apartment size it would be my absolute, orgasmic utopian paradise.

After a year and a half of renovations, my petite sky-castle was complete, all the neighbors came to take a tour of the place, or rather they wandered in while the contractors were there. Well, they couldn't believe the transformation. Everyone in the building was delighted; finally, the apartment could fit in with the rest of the building's units. And thank God they never saw my Capodimonte cherub wall sconces.

So, as I sit here in my mini-majestic living room, wearing my favorite silk salmon-colored floor length kimono robe with marabou fur sleeves – which is not realistic for typing, by the way – I take a sip of my morning drip coffee, look around and gives me a real sense of naches. *Which, for all the non-cultural Jews reading, is Yiddish for pride. My Grandmother is from Boro Park, Brooklyn - Yiddish is very much a part of "New York Italian."* But my naches doesn't come without the regular sharp pangs of melancholy. I lean forward, reach for my phone to switch gears to Barbra Streisand Radio on Spotify, adjust the volume on my wireless speaker and continue to write this book…

You see, my glorious Sanctum Sanctorum aka Love Bunny Cottage (It's official name, according to the ceramic plaque my girls and I painted and now hangs proudly next to the front door, alongside the small brass key hooks and a mother of pearl crucifix) was so named after my ex-husband moved out. But the LBC was created with him and was supposed to be our family home.

When I was married, Paul desperately wanted to move to a peaceful *cul de sac* in tri-state suburbia but I *insisted* on our tiny family being in Manhattan due to my work. I was working on Wall Street, 12-14 hour days, and once the children were sleeping, I went to work as a *(very new)* stand-up comedian. Many nights our nanny would return for a night shift and we'd head down to the comedy clubs where I was doing a five-minute open mic or stand-up comedy set.

Like other Type-A personalities, I'm intense and I give my all with everything I do. This all came at a cost – a gigantic cost – my marriage. I wish I could sit here and tell you, my dear reader, that life is a fairytale and you are your own fairy god person, but life is actually a journey made up of a series of events and decisions. And it's absolutely imperative to understand what you're doing and why, because the last thing you want is to have the unfortunate cloud of regret over your head or its nefarious cousin cloud called "*If I only did this… then…*".

Look, I'm not one to suck the romance out of life, but I got so focused up by the same dreadful "List" that gets so many of us:

- College, c*heck*.
- Career, *check*.
- Husband, c*heck*.
- Children, *check*.
- Home(s), c*heck*…

I followed the "normal" path. (And God knows why, I spent the majority of my teenage years wanderlusting around Manhattan, mentally preparing and planning for my show biz career, but I digress.) I followed the rules and owned it. And yet, before I knew it, I was swept up, uncontrollably, in the undercurrent of life expected and my personal life suffered and then I wound up on a stage in show biz.

Funny little thing about mental health? Right when you think you have it all, it comes knocking and tests us. And for a good bunch of years, I felt like a failure, like a real crummy bum. I dealt with on-again-off-again depression, the kind that makes me want to wake up, devour a bowl of pastina, a box of Good n'Plenty, 10 cannolis – all for breakfast and then roll over for nap time. The kind of depression that acts as a full-time bodyguard following you everywhere you go. It was there when I was awake, when I went to sleep… nightmares – it was always hauntingly there.

I realized the only place I was able to get away from my depression bodyguard was inside myself. That's where all the work had to be done. I had to think about who I am, what I have, what I did and most importantly, what I wanted. I did this all while not looking back.

Ok, I looked back but only to write this book.

Love Bunny Cottage
New York, New York
2022

THE RULES

Rule #1: Be Cool   24

Rule #2: Keep Your Shit Together   43

Rule #3: Let it Go   51

Rule #4: Completion is Key   56

Rule# 5: Make Your Presence Known   68

Rule # 6: Life is Not Fair   75

Rule # 7: Keep On Truckin'   77

Rule # 8: Make Your Own Luck   82

Rule # 9: Mind Your Own Business   89

Rule # 10: Ignore It, or Change It   96

Rule # 11: Stop Being Poor   104

Rule # 12: Get On the Bus   107

Rule # 13: Keep a Taste for Yourself   109

Rule # 14: Keep Going   111

Rule # 15: You Are Never Safe   115

Rule # 16: The Unspoken Role of HR   117

Rule # 17: They Will Test You   121

Rule # 18: These People? They Are Not Your Friends   126

Rule # 19: Get the Introduction First   135

Rule # 20: Always Respect the Boss   142

Rule # 21: Pay Respect to the Commission   148

Rule #22: Don't Share Your Future Plans   152

Rule # 23: Keep Your Ears Open for Advice   162

Rule # 24: Omertà: The Code of Silence   170

Rule # 25: Dress and Act the Part   180

Rule # 26: Never. Ever. Tell Them   185
        How Much Money You Have
Rule # 27: Use Your Imagination   186

Rule # 28: Don't Do Drugs   192

Rule # 29: No One Respects a Hoe   193

Rule # 30: Reputation is Everything   197

Rule # 31: Slice the Garlic Thin   200

Rule # 32: You Gotta Laugh   205

Rule # 33: There is Never a Right Time   208

Rule # 34: Take Care of Your Life   218

Rule # 35: Obsession Can Be   220
      a Good Thing
Rule #36: Go Where the Work is   221

Rule #37: Always Help Others   232

Murder? Panic? Heart Break?

There it was, the private message staring at me on a Monday morning: Facebook's endearing attempt to ruin my day. "Your father is on his deathbed. At a clinic or hospital in the city. Sorry."

It was from an estranged relative of mine. Yes, We're Italian and that means family – but there are limits. I took a sip of my warm can of breakfast seltzer that had been sitting on on my desk, and thought: *What the actual F*? Spam? Delete.* Then my phone alarm went off and I was like: *Shit. I'm late.*

It was 9:30 in the morning and I was already late for my fourth meeting of the day. Welcome to Wall Street. One good thing about working 14 hours a day is that it makes bad things easy to forget. Which is why we have Facebook. And Instagram. And TikTok. And Snapchat. And Twitter. And Linkedin.

The next morning, another message. It was the same relative: "Elyse, did you find him? No one knows where he is. Someone said he was at Gouverneur."

This was starting to sound less like a scam. Gouverneur? The clinic on Delancey? The mental health clinic? The low-income clinic? Wait. Is this real?

I immediately put down my cup of mushy oatmeal from Pret-a-Manger, closed my office door and returned to my desk. Not that it provided much privacy, both the doors and the walls were glass and pretty cheap. I was staring at one of the three monitors on my desk and, dragging the tabs over, got to work.

"Jesus Christ…" I muttered to myself. I hadn't sat down and had as much as a cup of coffee with this aunt in over a decade. I was not in the mood for this: I had engorged breasts that needed a pump. I didn't have time, either. My calendar was full of meetings about more meetings, which I could *not* put off because on Thursday I was flying to …Why was I going there again? Ah hell, a FinTech conference in Florida.

Oh, and then finally, come Friday a vacation – yay! Vacation with my husband and daughters – which would be our first vacation as a family of four. But, wait. *NO*, let me stop *EVERYTHING* so I can go on a goddamn goose-chase for some crap that's probably orchestrated by a catfisher, some pimply fifteen year old kid sitting in his parent's garage in Siberia.

As I was loading hospital websites, my heart was beating double time. *Okay, maybe this* is *real. My father? Is dying?* With the exception of two weird run-ins in Little Italy, I hadn't even spoken to the man in 15 years. But now he's *sick and DYING?* It can't be…

I did what any other self-respecting internet expert would do, I turned the World Wide Web inside out. Addresses, phone numbers, any public or private hospital records, PDFs, anything I can find. I *'control f'*'d the shit out of every backend source code page and got…. Nothing.

I called any hospitals I could think of, but none had any information on a patient under my father's name. Now, I realize that my next thought is probably not a normal thing for a girl to think about her father, but I can only be me: *He's probably under a false name, that shady fuck.* So, I hit the phones. Again.

THE THING ABOUT Wall Street is that no matter how fancy the headquarters or office, you never *really* get out of the boiler room, even in a very expensive piece of Manhattan real estate. Unbeknownst to me why they wouldn't invest in soundproofing. Yes, the chatter of boiler rooms sort of falls into background noise, but only until you have to call all over the tri-state trying to find your dying father. *Totally normal.*

Forget what I looked like through my see-through door, imagine overhearing *those* phone calls? "Hi, I'm trying to find my father at your hospital. I was told he's on his deathbed. Would you be able to check your inpatient records for me? His name is... No one by that name? Can you try this name? He might be under an alias. Yeah.... he does that from time to time."

I canceled all my Tuesday meetings and made calls for eight hours straight. I had admissions staff confirming his check-ins, check-outs, I was waiting for call backs... I was taking notes, crossing things off the list. I pressed some tech engineers I'd worked with over the years to do some internet magic that was above my pay-grade. My giant wall whiteboard became a spider web chart to connect it all together.

The whole time I was thinking: This is insane. I must be going insane. My father is only 64 and has three other siblings; if he's dying why no one would reach out to tell his own family? His children!? Maybe this is a hoax, some sick prank. Maybe there's a psychotic hacker perched in a Cold War bunker deriving pleasure by in-boxing randos telling them "Your father is dying."

I actually think we had a web security course on this last type of phishing scam. Maybe it was a prank... or maybe it wasn't. If it *was* true and I didn't try to locate him, I would never forgive myself. For all the effort an entire day of hammering the phone and the internet resulted in – *nada*.

That night I went home to our Battery Park apartment overlooking the Statue of Liberty where I ate comfort food; the baked ziti I'd batch-cooked the week before. Paul told me in that dashing accent of his that everything would be okay, relax, it was probably just spam garbage. I felt silly for making a big deal about it, but I felt better, much better. I was at home with my husband and two baby girls, aged 18 months and three years old. We were excited about our first family vacation as a foursome to Florida. We were flying out the day after next, on Thursday, so Mommy could speak that night at a FinTech conference before starting the vacay. Since I was scheduled to speak Thursday night, I didn't even think about canceling the trip for what might have been a social media scam.

In the office on Wednesday morning, I was starting to relax. I hadn't had any call backs and I was coming off that adrenaline high of the day before. I was now starting to believe that Paul had been right about the whole thing being a scam. Although, after skipping literally every meeting yesterday and trying to salvage what I could before flying to Miami the next morning, the adrenaline came rushing back for entirely different reasons.

And that is Rule # 6: Life Isn't Fair, just deal with it. You see, well, alright we won't make that aside just yet, let's find my father…

THURSDAY MORNING, we were off. Whatever fires I'd left burning at the office would still be smoldering when I got back. We got off the plane in Florida with me in a suit and, of course, strollers, car seats, diaper bags and all the other crap you *need* when traveling with young children. We picked up our rental car and headed to the hotel, only to stop at a side-of-the-road Mexican joint to change a blow-out diaper.

Paul was minding the toddler while I was wrestling with a squirming 18-month-old on one of those plastic changing shelves in a tiny restroom. This wasn't a regular diaper change but an honest to God blow-out, but that's okay, I've done this before; shit happens.

The maneuver gets tricky when the phone in your Loro Piana wool blazer pocket is ringing non-stop. Finally, I got my daughter's diaper situation sorted, picked her up and checked my phone to see a series of texts from my boss. *JFC.*[*] *Get me out of here.*

I got out of the horribly suffocating bathroom, dumped the diaps, took a breath of air that wasn't *that* fresh, but an improvement. I handed the baby over to my husband and said, "My boss is blowing up my

---

[*] Jesus Fucking Christ

phone, order us tacos for us and I'll be back in two minutes."

I hadn't even made my way across the dirt parking lot to the rental car when my phone rang again. I started cursing my boss, but it was a number I didn't recognize. After Tuesday, though, I knew I'd better answer it. "Hello?"

On the other end was the voice of the same estranged aunt who started this carnival off with that Facebook message Monday morning, "Elyse. It's Angela. He's gone." she said immediately.

"What? Who?" I said with an exasperated voice.

"Your father.. I'm so sorry, Honey."

"My father *died*? Angela, I'd spent all day Tuesday searching all of the hospitals and no one had any records of him being there…" I didn't even know where to start or what to say, "How did *you* find out? How did you get my number!? What's going on??"

"My son went to mass at Our Lady of Pompeii and someone told him," she said, speaking slowly.

I was in complete shock and horror, incoherent thoughts were zooming in my head, "Oh. My. God! Ok! Let me think.." I was talking out loud, but really I was just trying to sort out the surreal turn this week was taking. "...I just landed in Florida for a business trip. I'm going to come back to New York, I'll keep you posted. Is this your number? Omg. Okay. Wait. Is there a wake?"

"We don't know." Said Angela, "But, if anyone planned one, it'd probably be at Provenzano Lanza on the Bowery or Perazzo Funeral Home on Bleecker Street. Call me when you're back in the city." Click.

By now I'd forgotten about the texts from my boss. For that matter, I'd forgotten about the family vacation. I rushed back into the restaurant and told my husband. "Let's all turn around."

Paul took out his phone and opened the Delta app. I knew it was going to be chaos at home in Manhattan, and I had a lot of work to do: Find out where my father is, get those details, find out if it's even true, go on a manhunt for his *puttana* of a girlfriend and, well, then I'd Lose. My. Fucking. Mind. In. Her. Face.

You really don't want to do that around the kids…

I looked up at my husband and asked if it would be okay if he stayed with the girls in Florida while I flew home to take care of business. "Of course," he obliged. He felt bad leaving me on my own but he said when I'm done, he'll book me a return flight and we'll spend time in Florida regrouping.

At the airport I rang the two funeral homes and – *boom* – Provenzano Lanza Funeral Home confirmed a wake for the next day, then called my sisters and told them to come into the city that night. I knew we had to act fast. I did. Within two hours I was back on a flight to New York City.

I KNEW MY FATHER had a girlfriend – some washed up old broad from the Lower East Side. And come to think of it, I don't even know if she deserves the description of *broad*, because that term almost has a vintage stench of glamor to it. She was more... A *beggarwoman*. Anywho, they met back in the 1960's in junior high. She was a fixture in my family's Greenwich Village neighborhood who would hook-up with all the Italian boys while trying to suck her way out of poverty.

I know this because she actually told me. *What a class act.* Her name was Roseanne and she'd been with my father one of the two times I'd seen him in the last 15 years; down on Mott Street, in front of the old Saint Patrick's church. She was standing next to him, like a petite, pale muppet with orange creamsicle Fraggle Rock hair. And she told me all of her business. Which just goes to show you that being Italian doesn't mean you know the rules, this schmuck had zero concept of *omertá* – the code of silence. *We'll get to that rule too, later.*

Yes, my father and I had a thorny, distant relationship, but he *was* my father. So I had Roseanne's story cross-referenced with the old yentas in my family's Mitchell-Lama apartment building in the neighborhood. It turns out that she *was* as bad as all that, she put on a Grade-A phony bologna performance in front of St. Patrick's, making an overzealous sign of the cross every time her body turned toward the church. Then there were her bullshit reasons why my father and I couldn't go grab a cup of coffee. She stunk of schemes. Cheap ones. I got her number. Figuratively speaking, we didn't exchange business cards.

I'd *seen* my father twice in the last 15 years, but I'd tried to keep tabs on him and in his own detached way, I think he tried to keep tabs on me. When he and my mother divorced it was… horrendous. I love being Italian-American, but some of us? Let's just say, we're good at talking but not a lot of communicating. And my mother took it as disrespect bordering on betrayal that I'd have a relationship with my father after what he'd done to her. So, I just went back and forth between insisting that I could have a relationship with my father to "just keeping tabs".

My then-husband Paul is British, and those people have their emotions on severe lock-down. He'd wanted the four of us to fly back home together, but I insisted on going alone. This wasn't cold-heartedness but, being a Brit, he really couldn't emotionally handle a) *my* emotions, b) my family's emotions, c) any potential violence that might arise when a) met b). That, and he'd have spent the entire flight saying things like "Calm down, Lovely." Or, "Relax, Petal." And that was the last thing I wanted to hear. Besides, I had to sort out a).

On the plane I had a little time alone to write a letter to my father, which wasn't that little, it ran about 12 pages – before getting to New York and my sisters getting to my apartment late Thursday afternoon. *My God was this the same day? Before lunch I'd been changing a dirty blow-out diaper in the tiny restroom of a Mexican restaurant in Miami.* Once my sisters and I were together, well… just leave it to three Italian girls to get every piece of information about this charlatan girlfriend. Within 25 minutes, we had her phone number, address, divorce records and were printing out every Facebook and Instagram post with her and my father.

While none of us really wanted to talk to the woman, we needed to make contact because the wake was the next day. So, we found a nearby payphone – rare in 2017, but you could still find a few – and dialed her number; she didn't answer. *Of course.* Plan B was to show up at her house, so we waited til nightfall where I would ring her doorbell and fingers crossed, she would answer. During those few hours, my sisters and I sat and talked and cried in disbelief. I was the oldest of us, the closest to him and had the most memories of him. We were ragged with emotion, vacant by the situation but I knew as the eldest, I had to keep us all together. We had a mission: find out what happened, where the body was, and go to the wake to see our dad and say goodbye.

When 9 pm rolled around, it was time to go to the girlfriend's house. It was raining, the type of inconvenient bucket style rain, because *of course it was*, and we headed over to her East Village tenement apartment. When we arrived, I said: "I'll go in alone, you wait outside just in case something happens. I'll call you if anything happens. And then, come up and get me." So with a shaky finger, I rang the outside bell and she answered with a raspy, "Hello?"

"Delivery!" I chirped.

Click.

I rang again.

I rang 11 times, actually, and on the 12th she picked up, "Hi. Delivery. Can I come up?"

Click.

Ring: "This is Elyse, Michael's daught—'"

"GO AWAY!" she screamed.

Something wasn't right. The rain was hosing us down with occasional claps of thunder. We had one cheap deli-umbrella between the three of us and I started to cry. My sisters couldn't see it because of the storm, but it was an outpour of despair, desperation, loss. I needed answers.

I needed answers.

Serendipitously, a Chinese food delivery man appeared, leapt off his bike, buzzed up and opened up the steel door. I quietly slipped in behind him. It all happened fast and we forgot to wedge the front door open. *A mistake my father wouldn't have made.*

Rule #1: Be Cool

People are going to try to get a rise out of you. That's just what they do. Sometimes it's real, and sometimes it's just seeing what you are made of – doesn't matter. I was perfectly willing to let Italian Jackie Chan believe that she was leading, because that would get me what I wanted. But never, never let them know they've gotten under your skin. Once they find that raw nerve, they leverage it to get what they want. So how do you keep them from getting the leverage? Be Cool.

Inside, the floor was slick with stormwater and had a stench combination of old metal and must. There was no elevator and she was on the fifth floor, so I looked up the old, stained marble stairs and started climbing. Exactly 98 steps later, I arrived and knocked on her putty-blue colored door. What sounded like ten deadbolts unlocking came from the other side and the door opened. Careful not to let me see inside, she slipped out and was on fire. "FIFTEEN FUCKIN YEARS AND NOW THAT HE'S DEAD YOU COME BY? What the fuck you want?" she yelled.

Now, most people would be mortified and at her sheer volume and aggression, not to mention her poor grammar – "What the fuck YOU want?" Not me, my father trained me for moments like this. "Now that you've confirmed my father has passed, I want the details," I flatly said.

"He died five days ago," she mirrored.

The timeline wasn't adding up in my head. *Was he already dead when I was making my calls?* I needed to focus. I didn't feel like I had to answer her, but needed information so I decided to play the game and let her think she was leading.

"Roseanne, after my parent's divorce, my father was unreachable. My father hasn't kept in touch with anyone. His phone number constantly changed. And after having my social security number 'borrowed', our family cars were doused in acid by a 'crew of mystery men', exactly 64 ice-picked tires and 15 years of 'unknown' hang-up calls... I tried to get in touch with him. But, I was also scared of him. I *did* try, as you may have assumed from our run-in a few years ago."

As I was talking, I ripped open my backpack and pulled out a map of his whereabouts for the past 15 years, the social media postings picturing him, the address of his Pennsylvania hunting cabin –

everything. This packet was not only the recent work of my sisters and I, but also the handiwork of my techie over the course of my career. It's always handy to have engineer friends who can crawl the deep web to find information. I held the packet up for her to see and began to pull out pages.

She was flabbergasted at the 75-page stack of research. "My father has three adult daughters – you know this. He gets sick and you don't tell us? How about reaching out to me when he got sick? Did this come on fast? He was on his deathbed and you don't tell us? You don't think to tell *anyone* in his entire family? Not his sister, his two brothers, cousins - no one? You don't find this a bit bizarre? You're not even his WIFE." With each passing broken sentence, I was losing control. My fists clenched, my voice became strained, my face red and my mouth started to chatter.

In the hall, here was this nasty woman looking dead in my eyes: Sixty-five years old, five feet tall, with her disorderly mop of hair and her translucent skin - *that might be attractive with makeup* - and a hardened face that said, "Life owes it to me." She had the energy of a prize fighter, a viscous spring in her step. My back now leaning a few inches from the blue tiled hallway, she took one step and flung me into the wall. She was pressing me into the hard, unforgiving tile with her one hand on my shoulder and her other around my neck.

She was hurting me and knew it. "You listen to me kid – we don't want anything to do with you, we don't want anything to do with *your family*, so beat it! Get the fuck out of here before I toss you down these stairs." I was facing the staircase and I could tell it was a narrow deadly drop to the floor. *Marble doesn't give.*

In the last three years, I'd had two cesarean sections, and this last week had been no picnic either. I was physically weak and my nerves were making me weaker. I couldn't believe what was happening: *Tough, take no prisoners Elyse was being jumped by a 65 year old Italian Jackie Chan.*

Trying my best to maintain dominance, I told her through gritted teeth that I had records of her previous marriages, how she swindled money from *those* poor schlubs, and that I assume the reason she didn't notify family about my father – being relegated to a bed, and his eventual passing – that she was trying to scam the system.... Be the executor of whatever "estate" the man had.

My father ran cash businesses. It's not something I'm particularly proud of, but he didn't have much "on paper." He did have a very nice rental controlled Mitchell-Lama apartment, a pension with the Newspapers and Mail Delivery Union (NMDU) and a pension with Pepsi from when he drove a truck for them when I was a baby. He had his hunting property in Pennsylvania. He probably had some cash and jewelry too, but of course that would be long gone, vacuumed up by this leech.

While she held me against the wall, I told her my sisters were downstairs – standing in the rain, and if they see this they'll have the cops here so fast and she'd be thrown behind bars.

She backed off. And that was good because all I had in my pocket was the wine opener I'd grabbed from my kitchen before I left. This maniac could've had a gun for all I knew (*and knowing my father's collection, she definitely did*), but I wanted the details for the wake and needed to figure things out. So I played it cool, like her jumping me was no skin off my nose. I cracked a few jokes like: "I like that you're a tough broad. You're just the kind of girl dad would go for."

It made me sick to say it – but she was his girlfriend. I did learn a lot from my family, including my hard-to-deal-with-asshole father. Roseanne fell for the garbage and said, "Hey kid – you're pretty funny. You should be a comedian."

Little did she know I *was* a comedian, albeit a new one, and our favorite things are life experiences that we can take on stage. Although getting hurled down a flight of marble stairs wouldn't be good for my stage presence.

Roseanne reluctantly gave me the details of the wake. Although it's hard for me to think of her as Roseanne – she's just the Italian Jackie Chan, or IJC when that gets too unwieldy. I offered to pay for the service. She laughed in my face, hitting me hard with a cloud of stale cigarette breath. "We don't need your money. I paid for it. After all he IS, actually, MY. HUSBAND."

Husband? We'll see about that…

THAT SECOND TIME I ran into my father, I had asked about the redhead from the first run-in. He told me about her. It wasn't exactly dewy-eyed, his comment to me? "She was a real pig from the neighborhood" that he "bothered" with. But he would "never remarry" and "wouldn't ever marry her, even if it killed him."

And I knew he wouldn't. My father wasn't a romantic, but the man had his standards. So IJC was lying about "her husband," but she kept on, telling me, "Your father's dying wish was that no one knew he was dying.* But I'll let you show up to the wake for five minutes. You have five minutes to pay your respects and get out. And no talking! And if you don't leave when I say, I will remove you."

What does one say to that? Tell me, I genuinely would love to know. I can tell you what I was thinking: You don't scare me, you aging muppet. I didn't get a

---

* What a load of shit…

lot from dad, but I am my father's daughter, and he taught me to be cool, calm and calculated.

SAYING GOODBYE

The morning of the wake, I stopped by the funeral parlor to case the joint. *That's right.* By "case" I mean scope it out, do my due diligence before the wake. And there it was, my father's mass card, blown up and propped on an easel, by the entrance way.

It had been a hell of a week - starting with that cryptic message about my dying father, from an estranged aunt who only knew about it because she'd heard something from *her* son who'd heard from someone at church - and wrapping it up with a lunatic trying to kill me. Don't get me wrong here, I am and will forever be grateful to Aunt Angela who genuinely wanted to alert me to a bad situation concerning my father. But during the days of searching for Michael DeLucci, she was pretty helpless. My father was MIA, possibly dying or dead, and she used the opportunity to stir up shit about who is mistreating her or indulge in some first-rate hypochondria. But, her heart was in the right place, I guess. And she was entertaining – I'll also give her that; on one of our last calls, she said, "Let's see who showed up at the wake. They're lucky I'm not there… because I'd get my girl gang and we'd beat the fuck outta her. They don't know who they're messing with."

Angela *is* like a New York throw-back: rough and tumble, smoking, big hair, chunky gold chain wearing Italian girl. And she probably would have beat the shit out of *someone*, but to do that you have to actually show up. As it was, I had to pay to have her husband shipped in for the day after spending 96 hours on a goose chase to locate dad in every shit clinic, every hospital, only learn that the man was already dead while I was changing a diaper in a Miami taco-stall, forcing me to fly New York-Miami twice by lunch. And then, *then*, I was jumped by the Italian Jackie Chan while she claimed to be my dead father's WIFE!

I was still having trouble getting my head around what was happening. So seeing the enlarged mass card was crippling because it was the first physical confirmation I had of my father's death. It brought things home.

Again, I'm the product of my family, and that family taught me to compartmentalize my emotions. Which is pretty good advice.

What was peculiar about the chosen photo for the mass card was that my father was in a tuxedo. My father doesn't *do* tuxedos. He is a jeans guy, mostly. Date night he snazzes it up, and for weddings, dark suit and tie – no bow ties. This wasn't him. I knew something was up, things didn't sit right. I decided to walk around the corner to IJC's niece's house, whose address I'd found while draining the internet all week.

At this point I was probably tumbling fast into severe PTSD, so you'd think that showing up at my father's girlfriend's niece's home was strange at the time? No. Fuck that. There I was. The niece's name was Jennifer and according to her section in that 75-page file I'd been waving at IJC the night before, she was about my age, a stay at home mom and had a penchant for make-up. The whole clan lived in these $80 a month walk-up tenement apartments. I climbed the four flights of steps and rang the bell.

Ding. Dong.

A lovely zaftig lady swung open the door and asked "Can I help you?" I could tell by the fact that she immediately opened the door without demanding who it was first that she was the babysitter. I could also tell that she wasn't from New York, she was way too nice and way, way, too trusting. I put on a face and said, "Hi, I'm a friend of Jennifer's, is she home?"

"Oh god no!" She blurted, "There's been a death in the family! The wake is in a few hours; Jennifer is out running errands. Try her in a few days."

I thanked the lady and went home to prepare for the wake.

What do you do to prepare for your estranged father's wake with only three hours? The first thing I did was beg my mother to go through any old photos she had of dad. And because this Coney Island funhouse of emotions wasn't enough, she was both furious and disgusted that we were taking the effort. Now *she* was betrayed. I'd have to put a pin in that one.

We went to the CVS to blow up the pictures and have them printed out. My sisters and I sat on the corner of the photo department gluing printed photos to big sheets of oak tag and writing in sharpie things like *"we love you daddy"* and *"rest in the sweetest peace"* and whatever else came to mind.

The next stop was to an old army navy surplus store on St. Marks Place where we bought a camouflage hunting hat and some pins and patches they had in big fish bowls by the register: A red Mack tractor trailer, rifles, and my sister's and my initials 'E', "A" & "G." We glued them all over the hat and just as I was about to pay, I saw they had a bullet casing made into a keychain at the register. I took that as well and pinned it on the hat. With our frantic, unconventional shopathon was over, we waited like lost souls at the corner of 2nd Avenue and 1st street for our bodyguard.

Yes, bodyguard.

Look, I didn't know what to expect when I heard about the passing of my father. What I *did* know was that I wanted to take care of any and all funeral arrangements if something wasn't already in place; and if it were, I was going to be there come hell or high water. But, I was scared too. You've met my father's girlfriend. I was scared for my sisters' and my safety.

During their divorce, my mother had hired a private investigator called Tony the Snake*, but Tony was dead and therefore was of limited value. I had to turn to the family.

Aunt Angela was married to my father's older brother, Rocco. They weren't estranged from my family because of a fight, you understand, but that they'd just sort of faded away. When I was 15, Uncle Rocco got a job in California where they relocated, but kept the apartment in New York. We saw them a lot less, and then two years later, when my parents got divorced, they just disappeared.

My Uncle Rocco was 6'5 tall and very intimidating. He was on an elevator union job in Oklahoma at the

---

* Yes, that was his name. For the record, he probably had a last name but who in that line of business goes by last names?

time. I got in touch with him and asked him to come to New York to be our bodyguard. At first he declined, he said he wasn't feeling well as he'd caught hypochondria from Angela, and couldn't make it.

So I begged him. And kept begging, I wouldn't stop calling, but it wasn't until I texted him a picture of a round-trip first-class ticket into New York that he obliged. It was a mix of my desperation, relentlessness and his not having to spend a dime, but it worked. He texted back, "Fine. Meet me on the corner of 2nd & 1st at 4pm."

It was 3:55pm, my sisters and I were all dressed in shades of black, nervously waiting until we saw him coming down the street wearing black snakeskin cowboy boots, black slacks, a crisp white button down top and a black leather jacket. All he said was "Let's go."

We walked a block and arrived at the funeral home where the wake had just begun. Rocco did a quick check of the surroundings and told us to follow him in, not to say a word and to follow his lead.

Once inside, my father's psycho five feet tall girlfriend looked up at Uncle Rocco's commanding stature, jumped in front of him and said, "Well. Well. Well. Look who it is! And what do you think *you're* doing here?"

He took off his aviator sunglasses, took her by her upper arm, pushed her off to the to the side and came straight to the point, "Move the fuck out of our way." Then he turned to us and said: "I'll be watching, standing in the back. Go do your thing and then We're out."

The room was a traditional funeral parlor set up with the casket at the front and modest floral arrangements on either side. They looked like they might've been made from deli flowers – or even recycled bouquets. Our arrangement was the largest one, a four-foot enormous heart made out of perfect white roses with a large blue sash across the heart's chest that read "Daddy." It was tucked in the corner and was turned backwards for no one to see. *Because that's a normal thing to do.* In front of the casket was the kneeling bench and a few feet back were the rows of chairs.

My sisters sat in the folding chairs in the back, but I felt I had something to say to the man; I had my 12-page letter I'd written the day before in my pocket. I crossed the room with IJC watching and then following me to his casket. I knelt down, staring at the body of my dead father. It was one of those moments where I saw what I'm looking at, but my insides were vacant with shock. I had both hands gripping at the edge of the casket with my fingertips touching the inside polyester fabric. And found myself thinking *Really? No silk?*

My father was handsome growing up, like Tony Manero. And as he aged, he had tanned, slightly wrinkled skin, salt and pepper coiffed hair and jet-black eyebrows. I couldn't believe that this was my dad laying here in front of me, inside a cheap box, lined with cheap fabric, in a room full of strangers.

I kept sticking my neck lower into the casket, squinting my eyes to study all of his features, the cracks of makeup, the cold lifeless body of a man who had so much unfinished business. I had a lot of talking to do, so I unclenched my grip and slid my hand down the side of my black blazer, reached into my pocket and pulled out a folded wad of scribbled-on loose leaf. Quietly unfolding the papers in a dazed stupor, I leaned closer and, in my incredulous and ragged state, started to read, saying the things I'd have said if I had made it to his deathbed in time.

I felt a presence next to me, I lifted my eyes from the paper and gazed into my father's face without turning my head to see who it was. I didn't need to, I felt her hot, hellish breath of the IJC blowing in my ear. Raspy, gravelly voice started to hiss in my ear, "I told you no talking - time to leave."

I ignored her, lowering my eyes back down to the paper and with a slight pang in my heart, started reading again, "Dad... Remember when we went..."

"I'm not going to move," she hissed.

"Dad..." I said quietly to my father, "please make this stop..." I got through three more pages. *Eight more to go.* My right shoulder began to twitch as I kept whispering my writing to his lifeless body in front of me.

She was back on my right side, and this time she leaned toward me and I felt her frizzy hair graze my cheek. In a gruesomely perverse way, she opened her mouth near my ear, and like a venomous snake hunting prey, she ran her tongue alongside the cartilage of my ear, "I'm not going to tell you again, to leave." She hissed, "You don't belong here."

I gave it a moment's reflection, remained in place and tried to ignore her as a tear rolled down my left cheek. I refused to give her any respect or acknowledgment, this was my time, *my only time, my last time* and I was going to power through the remaining pages.

With '*mindfulness*' out in the zeitgeist, I tried to stay present in my last moment with my father, desperate to create a peaceful space, a second solitude, reflection and just trying to focus on the bigness of the situation. I wasn't just an adult child talking to her deceased parent; I was someone who was trying to make up for lost time, finish business, and cope with the fact that this monster robbed me of being able to pray, hope, and send my father's soul into heaven.

The entire time I was kneeling, trying to remain composed and gather my thoughts, IJC stood one foot away trying to intimidate me. Every thirty-seconds, she would come closer with that stale cigarette breath and her shoddy capped back teeth. *Is that aluminum capping? Ew...* Then She'd whisper something in my ear. It was unfathomable, but it was there. When I got to the second to last page of the letter, my sisters, who were sitting in the very back row of the parlor, yelled out with a pang: "ELYSE! Please! Come Here."

Now I was getting it in stereo, but I refused to turn. Without listening to any voice that wasn't my own, I finished my letter, put my hand into the casket and I gently stroked my father's cheek. "I love you *and* I hate you for being such an asshole the last decade. Please watch over us, Dad. Please."

When we'd come in, no one was there except IJC, my sisters and Uncle Rocco, so I knew the front row of seats were empty. Using the edge of his casket to pull myself up, I took ten lifeless steps backwards and gently sat down in one of the front row folding chairs. I slumped forward and hung my head down with shame. Not for me, but for the whole fucking mess; it was shameful that this man had lived for 64 years only to have a con-job of a wake with none of his family there. There was also a personal shame – of the particularly annoying *tsk tsk* type – if we, as a family, had just functioned properly in a *post-divorce-people-make-mistakes-so-move-on* sort of world.

It was a horror.

There I sat alone for all of a few minutes until I saw two small feet in front of me and felt IJC's small, cold presence. She put her hands on her knees, leaned forward to my face and said: "You don't listen, do you? You had five minutes here. And you abused it. I told you not to speak to him. And you spoke. Go now. Before you know what's good for you."

With my head down and puffy eyes staring at her cheap pleather black boots, I slowly picked up my head as if it were a bag of cement bricks, my eyes looked directly at her through their swollen slits, and with an emotionless *sotto vocce*, I said, "Get away from me. Or I will drown you further into poverty with legal paperwork."

She stood up and stomped off screaming, "I'm calling the cops! Where's the fuckin' funeral director? Where is that prick? I swear to God. Get these kids outta here." Then she turned back at me and snapped, "I paid for this. It's *my* room." *My father was right - total pig.*

As she'd stomped off, a girl my age came and sat down next to me. "Elyse… I'm Jennifer. Roseanne's niece." She was plump, about 5'7 with a Kohl's meets Dollar tree fashion sense, and she was a pawn in this charade. "I have your picture." I muttered, "I know who you are."

I kind of felt bad for Jennifer; her parents had passed away and been raised by Roseanne, so she had been a part of my father's life. Most of what she thought she knew about my sisters and me she got from her aunt. And, I think that having actually met me, a daughter grieving over her father in a *sort of* normal way, freaked her out. After sitting next to me for a good couple of minutes, she said, "I just want you to know that your father always spoke about you. He didn't know how to use the computer, but he'd ask me to "look you up" and he'd spell your name. He'd want to see where you were working, and he would watch any video clips I'd find. I mean, I'm not supposed to talk to you… but… but… I just thought you should know that."

IJC reappeared and said, "While the cops are on their way, ya got no business being in the front row. That's reserved for *family*. Get in the back row where you piece of shits belong." And then to her niece, "and you - shut your filthy trap." *Wow. What a classy lady.* I thought.

I got up and I walked to the back row of the funeral parlor and took a seat. My sisters had run out the door in hysterics. I heard my younger sister scream from the street outside, "Why is she in there? Why is she letting them abuse her? Someone help her!"

Stoically, I sat in the corner back seat without taking my eye off my father. I wasn't going to rush my time and I didn't want any more of a spectacle. I'd stay composed now and when this nightmare was over, I'd handle her.

Rule # 2: Keep Your Shit Together

Keep your shit together no matter how trying a situation is. Collect yourself: your thoughts, emotions, actions. Button it up, tie it with a bow, throw some glitter on it. Do whatever you need to do to stay on course.

For about 20 minutes, Roseanne's straggler friends came in and I sat there watching my father who, were he alive, would have closed his own casket top by now, as he hates this kind of commotion.

The director of the parlor approached uncomfortably and said, "First off, I'd like to extend my condolences. And I don't want to do this, but the deceased's wife is causing me a lot of problems and has called 911. So, before the police come, would it be ok if you stepped outside? You can come back in between the two wakes and have your time alone, I will open the doors up for that…"

"Do you know who I am?" I asked.

"Well, no…" the man said, "she said, you are long-distance relatives, but not welcomed."

"Do you have kids?" I asked him, teary eyed.

"Yes, I do. I have kids."

"Your own kids? Like, you're the father?"

"Yes, they are my kids."

"Your kids would be devastated if you passed away… I mean, you're their father, right?"

"Devastated is an understatement."

"Well, that's *my* father. And those two other girls? Those are my sisters, also his daughters.

"And 'my father's wife?' She's *not* his wife, she's his girlfriend. Who, I assume, tried to marry him on his deathbed. And the tuxedo 'wedding' picture of father blown-up on the easel? The insulting $14.99 flower arrangement that says 'for my husband' over there? It's a front, a scam.

"I know that because I requested his death certificate and under spouse, it says, 'fiancé'; I also arranged down at the courts, that should this certificate be changed in any capacity that I – me, the next of kin, the 'executor of whatever estate' he has – is to be notified. And the courts obliged. My apologies for the long-winded answer – I just thought you should know who I am."

I didn't move. My legs and arms were folded and my sunglasses down. The director of the home stood in front of me with a blank stare on his face. Up front, IJC would look back and periodically screech, "What's goin' on back there!?"

Uncle Rocco popped his head in. "Shut the hell up you, old broad."

The director, desperate for calm, whipped his head around, "Ma'am please, I'm taking care of it." Then he turned back to me, "So what do you want me to do?"

I cleared my throat, "By law when someone is waked, I believe you're supposed to ask for proof of documentation that this person is the legal spouse. I'm going to assume that you didn't get a copy of a marriage certificate when this was booked. I'm also going to assume that she read you the old riot act… she's 'one of us, Italian…' a permanent fixture of the neighborhood for decades. Maybe she even leaned on her own health issues? Apparently, she's been dying of lupus for the past 50 years.

"So, what I'd like to happen is for you to make sure my father is buried with this letter in his blazer pocket. And this picture of my sisters and me. I also want the details she planned for the funeral, and when this is all over, I'd like to have a sit down to go over the paperwork from when this was booked. If you agree to this, I'll go in peace."

"Ok," he said, staring in both confusion and relief.

On the way out, some old man from the neighborhood tapped me on the shoulder and said, "Kid. You're a dead ringer for your father. Come back to the night wake, the NMDU union will be here and there's some money coming to him, that should go to you and your sisters."

I never bothered going back to the evening session; I had my peace, and I left on my terms.

THE FUNERAL WAS the next day. No one sat on the family side of the church except my sisters and myself. On the other side, were the sporadic acquaintances of that shitty girlfriend, her niece and some old timers from the neighborhood. You know the ones: their sole pastime is going to neighborhood wakes and funerals.

The priest gave the eulogy and it was not the stuff of poetry. All he said was "This man…drove a truck. He drove a truck and delivered the news." To pad it out a little, he repeated himself five times. It was pathetically sad, lacking in words, quality and devoid of any personal affectations or memories. It was as if I were attending a service for a homeless man without family. *Which maybe in some ways he was…*

When the organist started playing "Ava Maria" and I gasped with uncontrollable sobbing. In retrospect, I should've walked up to the pulpit and given a heartfelt, off-the-cuff speech about the father I'd had until it all came apart when I was 17. The father who drove me all over the place, who taught me how to shoot rifles and shotguns, who always watched John Wayne westerns. The father who encouraged my creativity; my painting, drawing and writing. And, maybe I could've even filled more airtime with a Ted Talk style-eulogy on how we make mistakes in life but we shouldn't be held on a cross for them... and how even though we can't erase our pasts.... and no matter what, even if marriages go sour, the children – adult children – only get two parents.

I didn't do that. I don't know why; I just was not in a terrific state of mind. As the "Ave-Maria" played, two more people joined our side of the church. It was an older male gay couple channeling a Liberace vibe: Ass-less chaps with a touch of Elton John. You know the look. They were absolutely fabulous – a real relic from old downtown New York. They lived in the neighborhood and adored my father for his hunting stories. One of them whispered to me: "We loved your dad. He never judged us. He was one of the cool street guys."

And that was my father's funeral – almost exclusively attended by con artists, estranged daughters, and a marvelous gay couple that puts everyone from Andy Cohen to the Village People to absolute shame. *Sorry Andy. Love you.*

I just wish that had been the end of the episode. The altar boys were doubling as pallbearers – whatever. As they carried the casket out, I insisted on walking directly behind it. No one – No. One. – was going to get between the casket and me. I was hovering on the toes of the back pallbearer, and when we only had a few steps to the church's exit, I heard the niece Jennifer behind me whispering, "Please stop, Aunt Roseanne. Let them be. Please don't!"

I clenched and before I knew it, I heard, "The hell with them. HE'S MY MICHAEL!" She *flew* through the air and …*THUD.* The woman and her electric hair landed on top of the casket and started screaming "Not my Michael. Not my husband. Nooo!"

Eventually, she rolled herself off and the pallbearers loaded the casket into the hearse. Then, as she walked away, I shit you not, she laughed and lit up a cigarette. I went over to her and said, "Take a good look at my face and don't forget it." And walked away.

I guess the joke was on my sisters and me because IJC and the hearse managed to lose us on the Brooklyn-Queens Expressway. Instead of proceeding like a civilized funeral procession, it was like the O.J. Simpson chase on the 405.

The cemetery was in Queens, Cavalry, and it is literally humongous – the largest in the United States; 365 acres with over 3 million burials. Of course, IJC picked this overcrowded maze. We looped around the green grass, headstones and mausoleums trying to find these savages, these devils in the flesh. We couldn't find them until we heard a screech of a minivan peeling away. To our left we saw a freshly dug grave with large sheets of plywood half covering it. I took my backless cowboy slides off (paying fashion homage to my dad) and ran barefoot to the grave.

There were no flowers; it wasn't even my father's plot. It was a horrid shared plot she apparently had access to, probably pulling the same Grieving Wife nonsense with the cemetery that she'd pulled at the funeral home. *His name wasn't even on the headstone.* And the placement was particularly disgusting, as it was about six feet from the shoulder of the noisy and congested Brooklyn Queens Expressway.

I laid down on the ground and with all my might, I pushed the plywood off the top of the grave and I saw my father's casket. Just dumped in the ground, not even lying flat, at a crooked tilt. "Just a 'dump the body and run' sort of situation." I told my sisters. "I'm goin in!"

"WHERE?"

"In the ground! I'm going to fix the casket so it can lay flat."

"ELYSE! Please you are not in your right state of mind. DO. NOT. JUMP INTO A GRAVE. YOU CAN'T MOVE IT. I'M CALLING MOMMY."

The thing is, my mother didn't care. As far as she was concerned, my father was dead the day they split up. My parent's divorce, which I'll tell you about later on, was brutal. They didn't handle it properly; my father left the family physically and my mother, for me at least, left emotionally. She told my sisters and I we were disgusting for caring about his death and insane that we would even show up. *Disgusting is a little extreme, Ma? No?*

I calmed down and realized grave diving wasn't my finest idea. As a compromise, my sister agreed to "decorate" the gravesite with the eight dozen roses we had with us, taking the petals off the stems and throwing them into the grave, along with another short note I wrote and some photos of us. It actually looked nice.

We spent the next few hours in the decrepit cemetery office with me trying to negotiate moving my father's body into his own, respectable plot, with a nice headstone. They refused, telling me that those arrangements rarely happen and have to go through the funeral parlor.

It was a 96-hour whirlwind that changed my life forever. During the tumult, I clung on as best as I could… I barely survived. I didn't know if I was going to get murdered, have a debilitating panic attack or die from heartbreak. Or a combination of all three.

But I learned something.

Rule # 3: Let it Go

It happened, now move on. Or try to. A lot of people will treat you badly – don't waste too much time or energy on why, because chances are, they don't even know why – they're fucked up. Let it go and then live well. After all, living well is the best revenge.

One month later I went back down to the court to see that IJC, that con artist, changed the death certificate to *"time of death: spouse."* I have multiple copies of each in my safe to this day. I spent the next year dealing with lawyers on how I can sue her for fraud.

And then one day, I made a few moves that blocked her from certain things, but eventually decided not to proceed with a lawsuit. Because in life, our time is *so* precious. I had two gorgeous daughters at home, a thriving career and I didn't want to waste any brain space on some pathetic excuse for a human being.

God, It Was Stuffy in There

Be careful who you call your friends. I'd rather have four quarters than 100 pennies.

— Al Capone

The interesting thing is that as I've gotten older, these rules have come in very handy in life. Lucky for you, that is exactly what this book is about.

I was born in Bay Ridge, Brooklyn – ten days late. My Mother said it was a pain in the ass to which I tell her, "Ma, fine I arrived fashionably late but I came out of the womb in a leopard-print skirt suit ready to take on the world."

I was a determined Italian-American girl in a loud Italian-American family in a bustling Italian-American neighborhood. *Actually, the block I grew up on was Jewish - but that comes later.* And with that said, family is very important, even for the extended family, sometimes *very* extended family. Cousins were always coming in and out of the house - or at least that's how they were introduced, but I had my doubts. No one has that many cousins.

My mother's mother was called Nonni – a woman with eggplant colored hair sprayed and shaped into the shape of a, well, eggplant. Yes, she basically has a piece of produce on her head. She dressed in mostly big cat prints and always walked around on her red rhinestone cane. She would share her accumulated wisdom from her age and our close-knit culture. "They're not your friends." She'd say, "They'll never be your friends. They'll stab you in the back in a heartbeat. Don't trust anybody."

To most, maybe mildly frightening, but to me? Enchanting and endearing. Besides, you don't know my Nonni. My grandmother is a Boss in her own right. My mother's parents were both Brooklyn-born, first generation Italian-Americans. Anne and Arthur, or as I lovingly call them, Nonni and Poppi, had a successful fabric import business. They also shrewdly bought Brooklyn real estate in the then-sleepy neighborhoods of Park Slope – *when it was all Italian* – and Gowanus – *when it was just a canal filled with raw sewage and dead bodies.*

When my grandfather died at the young age of 58, in the early 1980s, Nonni was left to run the real estate business alone. As a woman in her early 50s and now newly appointed landlord of real estate, the male business owners showed her zero respect.

So, she demanded it.

It's not the sort of thing that you can mandate with words. *That never works.* Nonni's approach was a no-nonsense attitude, speaking little and visiting the properties unannounced with bodyguards. That's how she demanded respect. And that's exactly what she got.

But of course, like all miserable New York real estate stories, she sold off all of the properties in the late 1980s because it wasn't worth the *agita*. Still, in those few years of running a "man's business in a 'man's world", she incurred a lifetime of Boss wisdom. And let's be serious, she was always the Capo. She was the Chairwoman and she let my Grandfather be the CEO.

When I was three years old my mother and I were visiting Nonni at her house on the water in Mill Basin, Brooklyn for Sunday dinner, which meant around two in the afternoon. We sat downstairs in the dining room and as usual, all the doors were locked.

A typical Sunday, huge meal of macaroni, meatballs, sausage, braciole, loud talking or shall I say - talking over one another; overall, just your average family enjoying life. One small issue, unbeknownst to us, someone picked the front door locks, disabled the house alarm and walked through the door and upstairs to rob my grandparents of everything in their bedroom: Jewels, money, even the TV. *Who the hell can carry a 1986 wood-paneled television set?*

I'm sure this guy walked right out the same way he came in. *I hope he got a hernia.*

The experience only confirmed Nonni's depression-era fears and anxieties and she added another often-repeated quote to the earlier one: "Nothing is ever safe." Thirty-five years later, Nonni is still convinced that it was an inside job.

What kid knows what's an "inside job?" To me, of course it was an "inside job," they broke *inside* the house and took everything *outside*. The older I got and the more times I heard the story, I thought: safety, even when you're with your family or employer, isn't guaranteed.

MY MOTHER WAS ONLY twenty-one when she and my father got married in 1981, and gave birth to me at twenty-three. She went to New York City's Fashion Institute of Technology (FIT) for college and, after a stint working in public relations and hating it, decided to become a nurse. Throughout my childhood, she was going through nursing school, receiving her Master's degree, becoming a RN, NP and eventually even studying for her PhD; although she never finished it. *Ugh.*

Rule #4: Completion Is Key

Did you know our brains tend to remember unfinished tasks rather than completed ones? It's a thing. An actual phenomenon called The Zeigarnik effect. Basically, it means when something doesn't get completed or repaired, our marvelous human minds will continue to recall the experience. My point: Don't do half a job - if you start, let's just finish it.

My father, on the other hand, had a junior high-level education. By the time I came along, he had a CDL license and drove a truck of Pepsi. As the first grandchild on my mother's side of the family, I came with a very generous here-is-some-money-to-start-your-own-business-with gift. So, my dad set up shop in a shipping yard down in Red Hook, Brooklyn and began to operate his own domestic import/export trucking business. *Something like that.* I was never really certain what the man did.

No one really thinks through the particulars of their childhood at the time. You are too trusting, too naive, you have nothing to compare it to. So it was only in retrospect that I began to see that the mob, *La Cosa Nostra* (literally "our thing" in Italian) and corporate America have a lot of things in common. For one they are both, historically, male-dominated. And second there is a definitive structure, hierarchy, jobs to be done and most importantly, rules.

Despite what comes out of Hollywood, the mob wasn't born out of a desire to wreak havoc among WASPs, it is a business. Like any business, they care about money and power. And, just like corporate America, they get people to work together for a common cause, to do something for a common benefit. *And yes true, it is a business with a relaxed attitude towards the law, but it is very serious about its rules.*

When you are raised in an Italian-American family, the rules are everywhere. Kinda like Jesus has his 10 Commandments and us Italians, we got life commandments, which in both cases, serve as a code of conduct. There were things that we "did" and "didn't do." Take a simple example: Company coming over. When they come through the door, the first thing we do is offer them something to eat and drink. It's so normal that you never even think about it. Or at least I didn't – I wasn't a kid with a penchant for social and psychoanalysis.*

---

* That would come much, much later.

So, my mother and father would occasionally throw out nuggets of wisdom to my sisters and me like "Never tell anyone your next move" and "Never tell anyone your business!" I just thought these were strange things parents (and Nonni) said to assert their *parenthood* or scare their kids. As I grew up, though, I learned that they were rules for a reason.

WHEN I WAS FIVE my family made the move from Brooklyn to the countryside... Staten Island. Out of an apartment and into the 1980s Staten Island dream; a semi-attached house. The best thing about the move was that it meant a block-full of neighbors and soon-to-be friends - and a *backyard*. Which my family outfitted with cement flooring, a few tomato plants and the holy grail: a 12 ft round, 4' ft deep above-ground swimming pool. I mean, it was no Hollywood, but it'll do.

I hit those Staten Island streets like a hot-stepper, at least I tried to be. There was one small problem, and that was while I made friends with my boy neighbors; Atari and Battleship wasn't really my thing. I wanted to be friends with the girls on the block, and even at the small age of five, these *young polite ladies* pulled a Regina George from *Mean Girls*: "You can't sit with us".

Maybe it was because I was a kooky kid? I honestly don't know what put them off; it could've been my Chaka Khan-like hair, round tortoise shell eyeglasses, my froggy voice or the fact that I felt I should be on a stage and regularly recited lines from the vaudevillian musical, *Gypsy*.* In any event, I wiped away my tears and did what any self-respecting five-year-old would do: *Beg them to play with me.*

There were two little mean girls, trolls in fact, Jackie and Susanne. And these two were particularly brutal – only when they were together, of course. When they were apart, I was their understudy best friend. *Finally a role!* Thinking back on it now, I can't believe kids – little girls at five, six, seven – would posse up and actually leave another girl out. I couldn't believe that they'd do it to me (!). I was fun. I had toys. I had a pool. My mother had Dunkaroos (*when they were on sale*). We had a huge projector TV. My vibe was pretty much: "Wanna come over. Please? Pretty please? Oh come on! Ok? In an hour? Ok, I'll wait on the terrace and watch you play until you let me join in!"

At five years old, you might say I was completely pathetic, but I prefer to look at it as I was passionately ambitious.

When the two tiny trolls would get together, they would do wretched things. I remember being so calm and smooth in my approach, like screaming from the terrace, "Hi girls! My mommy bought me the big bouncy ball from Pergament! You wanna see it?"

---

* Music by Stephen Sondheim - absolutely delicious.

"No." The trolls would answer in unison like an unattractive version of the Doublemint twins.

"...But it's purple and so fun! *Aand* if you let me play, I'll give you my NKOTB Jordan playing card."

"Maybe later, okay?" Said one of them.

"Bring the card!" Added the other.

At this point, I was thrilled to delirium. Elyse had plans. So I shouted "MA, I'm goin' out to play later - if the girls call me!"

I'm not sure what my mother was thinking, but I can picture her shaking her head. If I remember correctly, I sat at the window and watched the outside for the next three hours. I packed up my playing cards into my pocket and ran down the peach-carpeted stairs, through the den, slid the back door open to grab my new bouncy ball.

"MOMMMM." I screamed gently. "Where's my ball?"

"In the back. Or In the front. Elyse! It's outside somewhere. I'm on the phone!"

Anxiety ensued. Twenty minutes of me overhauling our backyard also ensued: throwing sand buckets and BB guns through the air. I was on my hands and knees frantically dumping over everything from pool floats and foil pans when I heard the clanking and shaking of our metal backyard gate followed by the slapping of the vinyl woven flaps and little voices coming from behind me. It was the music that would impact the rest of my childhood and into teenage years, probably the reason I'm a comedian and definitely why I'm writing this book: A cacophony of little girl laughter followed by, "Ha. Ha. Ha...We got your ball. Quick, run!"

My little body collapsed on the sandstone-colored pool gravel and I felt my small heart sink. I didn't cry, I just felt the slump of my afternoon fun slide down the drain.

These girls would continue to torment me for the next ten years. Then they stopped. When we moved to New Jersey.

GO THROUGH THAT enough times and another sort of anxiety ensues, but I had my coping mechanisms.

I come from a family of hobby artists. My great aunt was an opera singer, my godmother is a painter and piano player, my uncle a painter; growing up, I saw people expressing themselves. Creating was my outlet from bullying – that's where it all started. When the trolls would taunt me, my little body was so engulfed with emotion that the only way I could articulate my feelings was by creating something. Happy or sad, a form of art expression will quickly follow.

So, at five years old and with no good girl friends, my mom set me up on a playdate who might suggest an activity other than torturing her scratchy-voiced eldest daughter. Basically, what I'm telling you is my mother wrangled up some rando so I could have a forced playdate with a new girl, Melissa Rothstein. I didn't *not* want to play with Melissa, I just preferred to play with the "cool" five-year olds on my block – the ones that didn't want me. You get my gist.

I didn't want to talk to her, let alone go to her house but at five years old, you really don't have a choice. Melissa and I were pushed together by our parents. So, with my big wavy hair swept up into a high-side pony, my champion tracksuit adorned with rhinestones and puffy paints swiggles (this *was* Staten Island in the 1980s), I reluctantly sat at Melissa Rothstein's plastic-covered dining room table on a playdate. And when Melissa's mom denied me of a sippy cup Shirley temple, I settled on the next best thing: Coloring.

Of course, Melissa had a nauseating stack of coloring books, everything from *Jem* to *The Snorks*. The thing is, I hated coloring books, I didn't want to "color" in someone else's drawing. Why? What is this, prison? I was completely offended. Why should someone get to decide what gets colored-in and what doesn't? Someone else draws the lines? Fuck that.

I *politely* asked Melissa's mom for a plain piece of paper, and that's how we started drawing hearts. Melissa wanted to sit next to me and I immediately broke out in hives. The problem was that my creative reflex is triggered at least partially by social anxiety.

And the trolls were making certain that I had some long-term anxiety. It also doesn't help that I have a nearly life-long aversion to.... people.

You see, when I was three, my mother trained me to get my own breakfast. She would pre-make me a cheese sandwich the night before and when I'd wake up at 5am, I'd pop up and go get my brekkie out of the fridge. I've been flying solo since. Some might say this is neglect, I prefer to say it was instilling the foundation for an entrepreneur.

This is a long way of saying, I liked to color alone. I mean, I was eating cheese sammies and jamming out to Fraggle Rock just hours before this forced playdate – why on earth would I want to sit *next* to someone and color!?

Melissa respected my chair preference. You didn't know me at that age, but I did; I'm sure inside my five-year-old subconscious mind, I knew the chair that spaced us apart was also going to protect me from her plagiarism. Anyone that uses coloring books is also the same person that will copy your hearts. Clearly.

We did not become BFFs.

I don't want to paint the wrong picture, I did have friends on the block: the boys. And we played the best games: manhunt, pick up sticks the day after 4th of July, and pogs (and I'd crush them with my metal hologrammed slammers). We stole strawberries from

Dr. Moo Keen Lee's office garden and had block parties.

Then there was the summer…Summers in Staten Island, we didn't go to camp, our block *was* camp. I can still smell, and vividly see, the start of a summer day. I'd wake up, bring my big bowl of Cocoa Puffs into the den to watch the *Glow Girls*. Then, sing and dance to *Soul Train* and when my dad would get up, we'd take an early morning ride to Sears. He'd fill a wagon up with drills and two-by-fours for a "house project" and when we got home, my day on the glittery cement sidewalk with sunshine beaming down would finally begin.

The best days were the ones when "the trucks" came around; the ice cream truck, the rides, even the knife sharpener truck. An old man would whip around the block ringing the bell, breaking every five houses and yelling, "Frank the Knife IS HERE! NEED A KNIFE SHARPENED? Only $1 dollah."

Me and the boys, we'd ring each other's bells, party all day, and nights didn't come for a long, long time. Each day I'd go to bed happy, sunburnt, freckle faced and couldn't wait to do it again the next day. We didn't have computers, or cell phones, so we made up our own games. And it was the best.

The truth is, even the trolls would jump into the summer fun when everybody was out. Typical cowards, they only turned nasty when no one was around.

I remember one day, maybe a year before we moved away, so I was about 12. The trolls screamed up to our window, "Hey Elyseee...Call the police. Wanna come out to play?"

Like the desperado I was, I yelled back, "Two minutes!" I can't recall remembering my Nonni's advice but I was so eager to make real friends with the trolls that I'd have ignored it if I had. As it was, I ran outside where they were waiting, grinning ear to ear.

"Cops an' Robbers!" They said, "YOU IN?"

"UM YES!"

They proceeded to tie me up with some string on the middle of the sidewalk, for everyone to see, and they stepped back about fifteen feet or so. Snickering, they picked up a handful of dirty rocks and said, "We're the cops and you're the robber. And *you're* in trouble."

And they threw stone after stone at me.

I nervously laughed until the impact of the small rocks started to hurt. I turned my face to one side, looked up and saw my mother peering through our cream-linen Venetian blinds. She frantically slid open the terrace door and started screaming in her long satin robe, shrieking in horror: "Elyse Elyse!?" My mother jumped down onto the roof of our family's Monte Carlo, and landed perfectly on the sidewalk where she ripped my arm close to her and said. "What the hell is wrong with you!?!"

Then she whipped her red teased hair around to the girls and roared, "I. Will. Be. Talking. To. Your. Mothers."

As she untied me, she kept repeating: "What's wrong with you? Don't you see they don't like you? Don't you see those girls don't want to play with you? Don't you see they are mean to you? Do you have to be hit over the head with a frying pan to realize this?!"

My lips quivered, I kept a brave face because now our older attached neighbors, Sal and Nancy, were watching. I shrugged helplessly and muttered, "God. Ma. It was just a game."

She ushered me into the house and said: "Wait till your father gets home. There's something wrong with you." Then she marched down the stairs and out the front door, to go to the girl's house where she demanded to speak to their mothers.

Honestly, she meant well, but it didn't really *help* my social anxiety.

Soon after that there was a horrific murder on my block; and shortly after that we moved away. I was bullied for those ten years, and more, into high school. But, what I try to remember most from my childhood is all the fun and laughter we had playing in the street. How the days blended into night which blended into weeks and months and eventually years.

The Italian - American Diaspora

"I learned nothing while I was in school."
—Lorraine Bracco

My family moved to Manalapan, New Jersey, when I was at the charmingly awkward age of 12. Ripe with braces, backne, and a voice that could kill a cow. My froggy voice now morphed into a mix of Fran Fine and ninety-year old Virginia Slims smoker.

This was a different life, a different world for me. If Staten Island was pseudo-urban, high school in New Jersey was vividly American Pie. Again, it was no Hollywood. New Jersey just lacked the style and panache of the boroughs of New York - *or anywhere*. I missed the eccentric personalities, the street games, and the food. This place was kind of, I don't know, *like oatmeal?*

We had the jocks, the cheerleaders, the nerds, the goths – who acted like a sort of misfit tribal catch-all which also included the then-LGBT community and everyone else who didn't have a group. I fit in perfectly nowhere. I guess if I had to choose, I fell somewhere in between the nerds and the misfits.

I was completely fine with it – I was actually delighted; finally happy to have a place to be accepted. No kid would ever choose it for themselves, but once it happens, there is a sort of liberation in not wanting to be friends with people who don't – or can't or won't – *get you*. I started to develop my own interests, and it wasn't to impress the local chapter of the Mean Girls. I was into Lisa Frank stickers, crafts, sewing, Barbra Streisand, Nathan Lane, Liza Minnelli, Joan Rivers, Amanda LePore, Louis Armstrong, anything that had to do with jazz, Shirley Temples, stand-up comedy, the 250-page Bergdorf Goodman catalog, and my obsession with interior design(ing) my room for when "my new friends come over."

Rule #5: Make Your Presence Known

As an awkward teen obsessed with showbiz, I needed a dramatic, ostentatious unveiling. According to my family in life, when we make our presence known, whether big or small, we gain power and influence.

My first day of school, my *Big Debut*, I knew I needed to make an entrance. I had visited my aunt's house, my mother's sister, who was particularly talented behind the sewing machine. I had envisioned the perfect first day of school outfit: A black ribbed turtleneck that my mother picked up in back to school shopping from Kids R' Us.* I had black patent leather chunky heeled Mary Janes that my Nonni bought me for $20 from WildPair†, and the *piece de resistance*: A skirt my aunt was going to sew a piece of my own design: A furry cow print mini.

You read that right. It was Betty Rubble meets B52 vibes all the way. Style Icon. Rural Americana here I come. And yes, New Jersey was rural to me. I don't think I saw more than one tree clustered together at this point in my life.

Like Cinderella and her Fairy Godmother, we worked through the night to make our custom couture gem; *Bibbidi-bobbidi-boo*, my skirt was complete. A thing of absolute splendor. The next day, I walked right into Mrs. Lewis' English class and, with the perky gumption of Elle Woods at Harvard, I said: "Hi I'm Elyse, I'm the new girl."

---

* Thanks Mom, that's a *real* popular seal of approval right there: shopping in Kids R' Us in high school.

† In exchange for me cleaning her bathtub 20 times, which I never did. Sorry Nonni.

There was a boy, we'll call him Evan, who was cute enough, and I definitely got his attention. He screamed out: "What is *that*?" Not quite the reaction I was going for – not a "her" or a "she" I was a "that." Not only a style icon, and way ahead of the future *what's-your-pronoun* normatives. I was "that." *I was all that and a bag of chips, TYVM.* As for Evan, he was a "he" and *he* later became my boyfriend. *Draw your own conclusion. Talk among yourselves.*

This pretty much set the tone for my time in New Jersey. Awkward with a side of uncomfortable due to my nasal raspy voice, which apparently was worse than nails on the chalkboard. *But*, that didn't keep me from talking; I was a happy, chatty creature. And as we all know, the slightest bit different you are in high school is pretty much the prerequisite to getting yourself picked on. None of this was particularly remarkable for American high school. I was a typical teenager going to the mall after school and when I wasn't doing that, I was writing my food and restaurant review column for my school newspaper: *Tastes Like Buttah.* And by the time senior year arrived, my wonderful creative writing teacher, Ms. Soback (who I credit a lot of who I am to this day), asked to be the editor of the school poetry magazine. *Look at me, thriving and living the life as a cosmopolitan journalist. Pure bliss.*

During the school week, I skipped out on cringy things like football games and basement parties and instead I took Manhattan – literally. I'd take the NJ Transit bus into the Port Authority and I'd meander throughout the city taking in the skyscrapers, billboards and business people and I'd tell myself: One day... I'm going to be living here and the only way they're going to get me out is feet first.

And my parents were cool about me leaving on the weekends for the city (probably because they were having marriage problems); they loved my idea of me making my Manalapan more bearable, so on weekends, I moved in with my Aunt Joan in TriBeCa. She was my dad's youngest sister, a legal secretary and my "cool single aunt." Every Friday, my father would give me $20 bucks, and my mother would toss me a bag of frozen Costco chicken nuggets and off I went on the bus. That was an amazing time of my life, being alone in the city at 17; I felt more connected with the outcasts in Manhattan than I did then in our new town.

I'd walk around on the bustling city streets, in my glory, listening to Donna Summer on my red Discman. While my aunt lived in TriBeca, the rest of my father's family were in Greenwich Village; it was my home away from home and I loved it. I would have marvelous adventures, in the city I discovered delights of matinee ballets at The Joyce, I wasn't much of a literary snob, but I learned I love a good bookstore and I'd sit and read the likes of Kafka and, when cockroaches would bore me, I'd page through the glossy coffee table books. I'd sneak into an indie movie theater – I loved The Angelika and Cinema Village – and catch whatever documentary they had on. It was a good day if some version of Bob Fosse choreography was playing. I went everywhere alone from smoky jazz clubs like the Village Vanguard to Carnegie Hall. I even visited museums; I really educated myself. At that point in my life, I think the only museum I'd visited was The Museum of Natural History. It didn't do much for me, nothing against Lucy, the oldest known homo sapiens, whose remains are there. She was a woman – you do realize that, don't you? The original badass, Nonni. I adored going to the Park Avenue Armory to the Antiquarian Book Fair, installation art at the random galleries on 27th Street. And every first Friday night of the month, the glorious swirly-shaped Guggenheim Museum would host a series called *Art After Dark*. Where singles would saunter with dirty martini and scoff over the long-necked Modigliani women.

I would shop all over the city; go into stores and talk to anyone that looked interesting, really. Some of my favorites? Pat Fields, Scully & Scully, Ricky's, Trash & Vaudeville. I'd hang out uptown on a Central Park bench and downtown on the sidewalk of MacDougal Street. Another favorite? Slipping into the Bowery Poetry Club for a game of "Tranny Bingo" which was the name of the event – just so we're clear. I'd swing by Velseka for a few fried pierogies. Hop over to Burritoville for a late-night bite. And then, I'd spend my nights at the Duplex and catch a campy comedy show. I loved all the Queens and Kweenz I met: from real to drag. I loved being alone, but what I loved more was feeling like I had a place in the world.

Spending time in Manhattan as a teen taught me that while I was picked on during the week, and didn't fit in with a high school crowd, high school was *not* the center of the universe - not even close. Manhattan showed me a world of independence, free-thinking and just doing your own thing. High schools in suburban New Jersey are pretty bland– high schools anywhere usually are. Getting away also showed me that I could escape any of my parent's domestic problems and drama that I was getting old enough to see at home.

Lemons and Limoncello

Other kids are brought up nice and sent to Harvard and Yale. Me? I was brought up like a mushroom.
— Frank Costello

Growing up my mother would sing me this song: *Life is Not Fair.. You Better Get Used To It.* She made it up. I hated it. Nothing like an Italian mom sharing life's sobering realities with her daughters. She sang this song all the time. Literally. All. The. Time.

In the Costco:

"Mom! Can we get this pack of super soaker guns?"

"No."

"Why?"

"Life's Not Fair, You Better Get Used to It…."

That sort of thing, or, I don't know… I came back from my aunt's one weekend when I was 15 and asked, sensibly: "Mom, can we buy a building?"

"What?" She'd say, "No!"

"Why?"

"Because we don't have money.! Life is not fair…"

"Better get used to it?" I finished the world's most practical duet.

Lucky for me, my contrarian streak took this as a challenge. If life isn't fair, then I have no choice but to make life fair. So that's what I did, and still try to do.

And in my mother's defense, she has a point. Although, whether to tell this on mixtape repeat to children trying to dream is another thing. Being quite so honest to dreaming children is like sitting them in front of a brick wall and saying: "You'll never have a water view, kiddo."

Rule # 6: Life is Not Fair

Life isn't fair. Life, as unromantic as it sounds, is a series of decisions, big and small. And with every decision, it leads into another road. Everyone gets a hand and we make choices: where we live, work, who we associate with, what we spend our money on – you get the idea… So, life is not fair and you better get used to it… True, it's a little harsh but it sounds better if you sing it.

Still, she was right: life can be unfair. I mean, people who are very religious – like my mother – might disagree, but by the laws of probability I had a 50% chance of having been born a boy. For that matter, I could've been born 400 years earlier, or born into a primitive tribe who thought a flint was cutting edge technology.

GOING OFF TO COLLEGE had been something of a (very) brief escape for me. I attended Temple University in Philadelphia with a major in broadcast journalism. Eleven short days after my college move-in date, September 11 happened. Like many, this changed my path in life.

My parents were already in the midst of a divorce, and along comes a national tragedy that takes away our beloved aunt, my mother's sister-in-law, Susie. She was one of the few corporate business people in my family. My Aunt Susie was the Vice President of eSpeed at Cantor Fitzgerald and lost her life in the towers at the young age of 44. Sheer devastation. I was seventeen and it was a crushing, overwhelming time for my family and, it goes without saying, the rest of the world.

I finished up my first semester at Temple University in Philly and I moved back home to Staten Island where my now newly-divorced mother moved to be closer to family. The whole situation was depressing, but I told myself the positive: I've returned to Staten Island, exactly 25.2 miles from Manhattan, and I'm going to carpe diem: *grab the city by the balls.*

I'd be remiss if I didn't say that my enthusiasm for being in New York was masking a lot of anguish. Obviously, beyond the state of utter shock that the entire city of New York was in after September 11, my parent's divorce was brutal. At the time, I actually didn't know *why* they got divorced, but when I came home my mother now lived in Staten Island, my father lived in Greenwich Village, and my aunt was gone. I was newly 18 and now living in some weird room in my mother's post-divorce rented Staten Island house. I felt completely uprooted. *I was completely unrooted.* But I didn't let this deter me, I kept on trucking.

My mother had a slightly different angle, she once told me, "You're only so ambitious because your father's not around." I like to think she meant that with love.

Rule # 7: Keep On Truckin'

Is everything one complete, full-blown, total catastrophe? An Armageddon? Did you die? I didn't think so. So, keep it movin baby.

I picked up school at St. John's University, did a semester studying abroad in Rome, and had four internships everywhere from major publishers like *Gotham* magazine to holding cue cards for WABC's *Live! With Regis and Kelly.* No hate on my alma mater but living at home back on The Rock, aka Staten Island, didn't actually scream *college living* to me. Actually, I was living in hell. That was one reason I was working so fucking hard – I didn't want to be there.

The issue was that my mother didn't talk about it with us, we never really knew what was going on. As for my father, he was a street guy with an eighth-grade level education, so he retaliated in the only way he understood, like an animal. He had people attack us, slash our tires and put acid on our cars. *Nice right?*

All the while, she didn't utter a word about the divorce to us because she didn't know what to say. She told me that my father is a liar and a cheater. She told my baby sister he moved to Africa for work. And that was the end of the discussion. Forever. Still to this day.

Years later, I did manage to find out the reason for my parent's divorce: My father had been cheating on my mother, and he'd been caught. To make matters worse, he'd managed to get himself in debt to the wrong people. One day three Nigerian men showed up at our door demanding money. When my mother found out, she shut it right down, and I mean everything. She immediately filed for divorce after 20 years and three kids. Game over.

I had a choice to make. I refused to let myself get dragged down into that disaster, no matter how much complaining or bashing I heard - and it was A LOT.

While I wondered if my own father was thinking of me and my sisters, I kept my focus on getting myself – and my sisters out of that Dante's ring of hell. What I mean by hell, is the dreadfully negative environment, that's only focusing on the past and puts way, *way* too much emphasis on "what we went through."

In the aftershocks of a national tragedy that forever changed America and the world. I was reeling from a series of smaller, personally intense family tragedies. I knew where I wanted to end up but I didn't know how to get there: I had absolutely zero family connections. My life seemed like a sour pile of lemons.

So, I decided that I'd make those lemons into Limoncello.

INTERVIEW IN THE BOILER ROOM

Great men are not born great, they grow great.
— Mario Puzo

My first interview was with a supermarket gossip magazine for an assistant copywriter position. *What a fancy title, right?* This interview consisted of a 20-minute conversation before they handed me a red Bic pen and a two-page, 2,000-word article that was a grammatical mess. My job was to make it correct and voila, I passed. The lady thought I was nice enough and I was offered my first job for $22,500 a year.

I was about to be rich. *Holy shit.*

I went to bed that night in my basement bedroom at my mother's newly purchased semi-attached house on Staten Island, dreaming about becoming Carrie Bradshaw from *Sex and the City*. Because that was the fantasy of literally every early-2000s female collegiate journalism major. Dream of being a quirky New York writer, thoughtfully tapping the keys of your white MacBook, all while sipping a cocktail and wearing a pair of Manolos inside your rent-controlled West Village apartment. At the time, I was reading this website called *ed2010.com;* it was a job board for college students that had the goal of becoming magazine editors by the year 2010.

I was on my way.

That night, I saw in my email an ad pop up (when those were a thing) for a sales and marketing role at a British publishing company. Under the salary field, it said: "$27,500 with potential to make uncapped 6-figure earnings." *Game changer.* Putting aside the fact that I didn't even know what "sales and marketing" was, I figured it since it was publishing, it was in the same realm of journalism. So, like that, I went from Carrie Bradshaw to the Queen Mum. I wanted the job with more money. *Pish-posh, pass me a crumpet, Philip.* That was the job I wanted.

The interview took place at a boiler room; a one hour-long interview and let me tell you, it went greater than great – splendid. But, I didn't get hired right away – can you imagine? But as a new graduate, what did I know?

Not much. I thought I was a big shot. My first company interview, got the job. At the second company, it went great so of course I thought, when I get the call, I know what job I'll be taking.

Guess what? They never called.

Two weeks went by, I stalled the gossip mag and followed up with the number on the business card of the British publishing company's CEO, an Australian named Mack Craven. When I heard his voice on the line I knew that it was game time. "Hi. This is…um… Elyse." Alright, so it wasn't a perfect start. "I was just following up on my interview…"

"Who?" Mack flatly said.

"Elyse. I came in about two weeks ago and interviewed for the 'International Ad Sales' job?"

"Oh. Righty-O. Yeah, we decided you weren't ready. Sorry, mate." It wasn't so much followed by a click punctuated by one.

RULE # 8: **M**AKE **Y**OUR **O**WN **L**UCK

I never really got "lucky" in my career. I focused. I strong-armed my way into opportunities, determined to make something of myself. Not to be someone that was just thrown away. Not someone that wasn't worth sitting down and nurturing when I was upset. I always had a relentless fire inside me and the fire grew bigger. I wouldn't stop until I got the same exact career as if I would've gone to an Ivy. And I did.

Did he just hang up? I hadn't put the phone down yet...Mate? What is this Captain Kangaroo? I thought to myself. And not ready? It said "entry level position." What does that mean? I just graduated!

I was very perplexed – and naive, too. I thought that when one graduated, they were guaranteed some job-offer variety. It was a blow to my ego. I was bruised. I put down the cordless phone, went back into my bedroom, and read the job description and salary again. And I said: "Fuck this."

I called Captain Kangaroo back.

"Hello?" Mack answered.

"Hi Mack. It's Elyse again. Sorry to bother you, do you have a quick minute?"

"How can I help you, mate? Everything Ok?" he said.

"No. It's not ok. You told me I wasn't ready for the job. And you made a huge mistake. Huge." I held my breath...

"Well...you seem pretty convinced. Why don't you come in tomorrow and we can have a chat. 9am ok?"

"Yes, that should work." As I was trembling with chutzpah.

I went into the meeting and, after we wrapped, he walked me over to my desk and I started the job that day. And it's a good thing because that's where I wound up meeting my husband.

Why So Many Rules?

You have to learn the rules of the game. And then you have to play better than anyone else.

-Unknown

That was just the beginning. I've gone on to other companies, had more side hustles than I can count, worked for different people on a variety of teams. It didn't take long for me to see that the corporate world wasn't that different from the world I'd grown up in. My mother and father didn't just say bizarre shit because parents are weird; they were trying to guide me because they knew that the world had rules.

And that's when a penny dropped, if I was going to do this right – and I *was* going to do it right – I needed to know the rules. I'm not a justice expert, nor do I want to be. I'm just a business person who grew up in a middle-class Italian-American family, guided by a set of rules that help me succeed in business.

Now, let's talk about why the world or any type of institution from families and conglomerates have rules in the first place: These guidelines remind people how to behave. They usually are clear, concise (hopefully) and designed to act as anything from commandment to simple reminders. When fair rules and laws are in place and enforced, they allow for peace and order. Without them, an institution would descend into anarchy, mass chaos and states of disorder.

When I got into business, a lot of these rules seemed very familiar from my upbringing. Very familiar. Understand that I'm not sitting here in Love Bunny Cottage in my impractical typing kimono, saying: Let's put the Mafia on a pedestal. I'm not. Besides, Hollywood already does a fabulous job of that.

What I *am* saying is the Mafia is based on family, I was part of a family and after we left the nest we all became part of other "families" which, in my experience, was going to work and joining a work family.

This is important because companies today are culture maniacs: They spend a ton of time and money on "company culture." For obvious reasons, they want it to be a place where people enjoy coming to. If we enjoy going to work and our employer has values that are consistent with the employees; this boosts the productivity level.

Happy People = Productivity = More Money.

While there are exceptions to every rule, we can say the same at home, right?

Happy Home = Upstanding Citizens*= Successful Adults†.

It is *Culture Economics 101*. These companies aren't just being altruistic, the revenues they bring in from this increased productivity, *way, way* surpasses the expense of free yoga classes and snacks. This is *so* important that they attempt to institutionalize their culture: When you join a new company there is someone that will likely give you a handbook, a printout or direct you to a page on the company website expressly telling you the rules. Telling you everything that you need to know.

Well, not *everything*.

Within every company, there lies *The Underworld* representing the inner-workings of an organization. The rules inside the rules that you will *never* find in the HR handbook. Your boss won't share these rules with you. Even your work wife and your work husband

---

* Mostly…

† Also mostly…

wouldn't dare to impart this level of secret knowledge to you.

Like most lessons in life worth learning, you just have to figure them out on your own, by keeping a watchful eye and ear to everything that goes on. And lemme say, if you think I'm setting this up as a bad thing, I'm not. It is simply the sobering reality of large and not-so-large organizations. It's the same everywhere, whether it be inside a large British publishing company, digital start-ups, Wall Street and, yes, the mob.

I'm sharing with you the rules of the Italian-American Mafia, these very rules that I learned growing up in my house, with my family. I didn't always follow the rules at the time , but in retrospect, I realized, I should've.

NO ONE IS PAYING YOU TO GOSSIP

No one gives a shit it if you're tired. No one gives a shit if you're hungry. No one cares. Just do your fucking job and hope you make it to bonus season.
– Anonymous

Fortunately, with my upbringing, a lot of these rules were just second nature to me. Things my mother or father had been telling me my whole life. Or Nonni told me after she'd stopped telling them to my mother.

And one of Nonni's big rules was…

Rule # 9: Mind Your Own Business

Do you know how much business you have? How busy your own life is? How much you have on your plate? I know, me too. Who cares about other people's business. Just keep your eye on Number One - that's you.

———

No matter where I've worked, there was always open floor office space and I've always heard fascinating conversations going on about affairs, fraud, food… I've overheard it all. Every single place I worked. Every one, starting when I was babysitting at 14. There I was hired, to watch some kid, standing with the mother in the kitchen as she frantically chops an apple on the Formica countertop, *no cutting board? And there was Gloria, wearing a gold sharp-shoulder padded blazer, high-waisted black acid-wash jeans with little ankle zips and spike stilettos,* having her blab to me about the "friend date" she was going on, when her husband was conveniently out of town…

Fast forward a few years, I've heard all the mishegoss inside the four walls of every skyscraper I've worked in. I can't talk about fraud, but the affairs... Oy. So many torrid love affairs. And do you know how many times I've been cornered in the kitchen being asked for advice? *Why me? What do I know?*

One time I had a corporate outing at the CEOs house in East Hampton because he had a 'big pool' ... *and really? Bathing suits? Seeing your swimming trunks and stretch marks doesn't exactly feel HR appropriate to me,* but there I was, swimming in a muu-muu and was cornered in the shallow end of the heated gunite pool "you think he likes me?" and with another swim, "you think my wife would find out?"

Ugh! These conversations happened more times than I care to admit. And what am I – stunad? I'd smile, shrug, change the topic: *Turn around your bathing suit is about to become undone.*

Am I going to lose my livelihood over scandalmongering? No! I need a paycheck. I have a career. I mind my business.

Money Talks...Loud

"No one gives it to you. You have to take it."
—Frank Costello

Early in my career, I'd hog up my therapy time with work talk; a classic deflector move but I was on a roll.. "It's not fair." I'd complain, "Sam is getting a promotion, how come I'm not?"

Dr. Long, my shrink, would say, "Oh Elyse. Who cares? Ignore them."

"Ignore them!" I was completely disgusted and insulted with this notion. I'd flail my arms up in the air like I just lost a court case. "How can I ignore them? Dr. Long, I'm practically a walking late-night television advertisement for an anxiety pharmaceutical." Is he seriously *and flippantly* telling me to ignore them? *Oh God. Someone grab me my velvet, rose-colored tufted chaise lounge and don't forget my paper fan, I'm about to faint.*

I became so accustomed to hearing the phrase "ignore them" that it sounded as if the Doc were coughing. I'd have a quiet acknowledgment of this bit of practical advice and then army-crawl back into my own head. I wish I did internalize it because God knows how many times "ignore them," became one of the most important sentences he uttered.

At work, there were tons of things that I wanted, of course there were! This was Manhattan – big time business and the world was my oyster, baby! Oh, I wanted it all: more money, responsibility, acknowledgment, etc... And of course, these things were, for me, absolutely impossible to ignore.

You know, when you acknowledge something you want, then continually dwell and kvetch on that *one thing you can't have*, disaster ensues. You've now put it into existence, made it real, given it credibility, validity and of course, spent way too much time obsessing about it. Basically, what I'm saying is: The more we pay attention to something, the stronger we make the thing that *you can't have*.

A lot of my friends will ask me my opinion on their own respective work issues. I'm no different from them. Which I can chalk it up to the fact that we all come from the same socioeconomic background, growing up in the boroughs of New York. It's usually my Staten Island girlfriends or some of the Brooklyn girls that I met at St. John's. And specifically, they'd confide in me about salary and promotions.

My best friend Victoria was working as a manager in the suites department for ten years at one of the largest event venues in New York City. She was miserably desperate for a promotion – *with a meaningful raise*. Each year, she received a 3% "cost of living" raise. So, after an entire decade of employment, she received a total of a 13% raise. Let's say Victoria works in the corporate world for 40 years. For one quarter of her entire working career, she's received a 13% raise? That's fucking bullshit. It's also commonplace. Happens everywhere, in fact, some firms argue that a cost of living adjustment *IS* a raise and something is better than nothing. And by the way, some employers don't even do this.

What I didn't like about Victoria's situation was that it wasn't the percentage points, it was the lack of value. In fairness to her employer, within these 10 years, she did get a promotion, she went from Manager to Sr. Manager to Asst. Director, but last time I checked, every time in Monopoly, when someone lands on Free Jail, they get to collect. So, she received promotions but no promotion with a meaningful raise. Anyone can make up a job title, but in the workplace *value is most often appreciated in the form of money*. Can you imagine how gut-wrenching those conversations with her husband were?

"I got a promotion!"

"Nice Babe! What's the new gig?"

"I'm now Assistant Director and have direct reports, but Baby? I didn't get a raise... They said I would *definitely* get one with the next promotion."

"Let's celebrate. McDonald's. On you."

Victoria was a VERY hard worker; she put her heart and soul into her job. She never took a day off, she shopped in Macy's career section like no one's business and always looked the part; she went to work with a miserable commute and a smile on her face. Weekly, she'd work way past office hours and never asked for a car home. And the best part about Victoria? She was the best damn Out-of-the-Office steward. There wasn't a family holiday or summer barbecue that'd go by that she wasn't raving about her co-workers, or new ongoings in the office. She was your ideal employee. And what did they do? Ignored her. And, she was just so desperate for that Director-level position *with the matching* salary, and she wasn't getting it.

And when she'd tell me this, my blood would boil. Sometimes after an espresso martini or ten, I would tell her, "Barge into your Boss's office with a pair of brass balls, along with a PowerPoint deck of your *year-over-year* performance, and ask him – *it was a him* – for three plausible fucking reasons why you can't get a meaningful raise. And if that doesn't work," I added,

"Go to someone at executive-level and ask them to vouch for you."

Victoria was sensitive and my aggressiveness would make her cry, so eventually, I changed tack, remembering the advice that Dr. Long had repeated like a mantra. "What you're going to have to do is ignore your desire for a salary increase, and when you're ready, pack up your shit, leave the company." Then, I continued, "Get the position with a firm that values their employees and show those bums what they lost." To this I added, "Murder at your new job. Absolutely destroy. And when you're killing the game with your Director-level title, if you really want to go back to those maggots who didn't value you - for a quarter of your professional working life, *might I add* - then make the case for it and do so."

They didn't value her and no one senior enough was vouching for her. And, I saw how the ladder worked with my very own eyes: Once Upon A Time, before I arrived at my company on Wall Street, at the very same company, there lived a Marketing Manager. Let's call her Jane. Jane was very driven and ambitious. Jane shared her ambitions with a Senior Executive; he took her under his wing and she swiftly rose through the ranks (with promotions and salary increases) over the course of fifteen years. Senior Executive made a case for her commitment to the organization and they decided were going to groom her for a C-Level role. And, what many companies do, and they did here, was they orchestrated her departure. Jane left and went into a new firm in a custom-created C-level role, she stayed for two years, and then came back to said firm and joined the C-Suite. The End.

RULE #10: IGNORE IT OR CHANGE IT

Lodge it in your mind and it'll grow powerful; if it's moot, better off ignoring it, or make the change to get what you want. And if both fail, ignore the rule and pave your own way.

This is different, way different, than Victoria's situation. This is a story of someone championing your career and guiding you through the process. Victoria was stuck in middle management, which so many of us are. Two completely incomparable stories, but I felt it would be appropriate to mention here.

Victoria shouldn't have given credence to her desire for more money, because there was *never more money coming*. And for whatever reason… Maybe they were cheapskates, maybe they were greedy heartless people;

regardless, she should've ignored it, made a game plan and got TFO.

The irony is that sometimes (not always) ignoring something can, in fact, change it. The less that you show that you're interested, the stronger you become. The more powerful you become, the more you actually, in-turn, get what you want.

Hobbies and Hustles

In the world of business, the people who are most successful are those doing what they love.
— Warren Buffet

This story isn't going to be told in an exactly straight order for the simple reason that I only found out something about my parents about two years ago, but it's relevant. When my parents were married, on weekends they sold comforters at Caesar's Bay Bazaar in Brooklyn.

"Comforters? THAT'S SO RANDOM." I asked my mother, "Why?"

"We wanted some extra moolah!" She said, rubbing her thumbs into her other fingers in the international sign for money. "We wanted some extra moooo-laahhhh." She really leaned into that last syllable to be extra clear.

I was totally bewildered that I'd never heard this before. I asked her, "Who gave you comforters to sell? You had a comforter guy?"

"I don't know Elyse. Your father got them. I think he got them off the truck." She said, "Lo Mein or Chicken & Broccoli? Now stop talking to me about that son of a bitch."

"Mom. I'm not even hungry yet. 1. He's dead. 2. What did you do with the money?"

"We used it to go out for dinner" she shrugged and walked away.

They made money and spent it. Sounds like what I did before I started working "real" jobs. The money mentality of my family was to work hard, make money, buy a house and live your life. We weren't one of these families that luxury vacationed; if we did go away, it was someplace drivable like Pennsylvania's Mount Airy Lodge or Ocean City, Maryland. I didn't know any other types of vacations were an option, but that's the beauty of being a kid, right?

That wasn't the money mentality of my entire family though.

My mother's sister, my Godmother, Teresa on the other hand, worked in mutual funds for big banks like Citibank, Dreyfus, etc.. She was wrapped up in the Peter Lynch-era of mutual fund finance. Compared to my parents, my aunt lived a completely different life; she traveled the world, as far as Singapore, lived in both London and New York where she owned a studio apartment on Manhattan's Upper East Side. My auntie, a name she insisted on being called after living in London, had the glamor and cosmopolitan life of an 80's power business woman.

With her small collection of tennis rackets, gemstone jewelry and a closet-full of skirt suits that would give *Designing Women*'s Delta Burke a run for her money, I would marvel at her life and think: *Do you need an assistant?*

I was seven.

As I entered my teenage years, I started to realize that the money mentality of my family and my godmother really *was* different, even if I couldn't quite articulate it at the time. Not that one was necessarily better or worse; my parents worked hard and spent money but I didn't hear much about saving. The only exception were the bonds I got from my communion and confirmation, which my mother deposited into a savings account and wrote the amounts down in the savings account's precious passport book. Opening up the possibility that at 11 my "portfolio" was in better shape than my parents.

Whereas, my auntie stirred on about investing and compound interest, and when she moved out of Manhattan and into Westchester, she kept (*kept!*) her studio apartment in the city, as an investment. For me, this was an eye-opener: she'd get a tenant in, have the tenant pay her mortgage and, I assumed, by time the place was paid off, Auntie could either have rental passive income or have her very own *pied-a-terre* on the glitzy Upper East. And that was it. I remember thinking, whatever she was doing, I was going to do. *Mirror effect fully in place.*

Eventually she married and moved to lower Connecticut, where she currently lives. She has one of those great barn-like houses; white with British racing green-colored shutters and great rolling front lawn, and right across the street, a yacht club.

Don't get me wrong, I loved my childhood. I didn't choose it, but I loved it enough. When I was starting to make choices about my own life, I wanted to be a part of making Big Cash —and doing it all under Big Lights but I couldn't be a starving artist because with my luck, *and my appetite,* I'd actually starve. The difference distilled down was this: My mother would say things like "*I can't afford it*" while my aunt would say, "*How can I afford it?*"

I may have wanted to adopt Auntie's money mentality, but I saw my father run his business. I saw my mother sticking up for me. I also saw her going for her PHD when I was in my teen years. All was, in my mind, respectable boss behavior. Crushing it.

SO, I HAD MY first job in a boiler room at a British publishing company inside The Fitch Ratings building at 33 Whitehall Street. If you don't know, a "boiler room" isn't really where they keep the water heater; it's a sales floor, fluorescent lights, lots of phones, no walls, no doors. Light on privacy. *I know you saw the movie* Boiler Room... Anywho, my job was in advertising sales and I had to make cold calls to C-Level executives and sell them a *(very)* expensive advertisement placement inside an "Executive Journal." It was a very elite journal, *so elite* that I never actually saw a copy of this illustrious magazine. I had no idea where the copies were or weren't hidden. Being naive, 21, and having a voice that sounded more like 41; I crushed the phone game and made more money than I probably should have.

I also realized I had the gift from God: *Closing.* And that is all I did. I worked the phone, sold advertisements, closed deals and every other Friday walked over to HSBC with my printed paycheck in hand – because that was a thing then – and deposited the *mooo-laahhh* into my very own bank account.

My first commission check was for $4,000. I couldn't believe it. I walked up to the teller with the arrogance of an inner-city rapper, slid my check into the teller window and said "This is a big one." I had no idea that was the start of my love for checks. I love a good check and, lucky for me, they got bigger.

The beauty of sales jobs? You can bullshit all you want in an interview, but make sure you close them.

Tell them to hire you, then tell them to track your progress and the rest is all you, Baby. Work your ass off, close deals like it's the air you breathe and then sit back and bask in your own success.

Although, you need to keep your head straight. No blowing the money – bad move. I was 21 and all my female boiler room co-workers had store credit cards to Barneys of New York (RIP). The girls would sit around at lunchtime and talk about how they "maxxed their cards out."

Thinking back on it, the whole thing seems insane now – and it was – but at 21, maxxed out plastic from a high-end department store had an air of glamor and panache to it. Now remember, I didn't have a ton of girlfriends growing up and my mother was frequently in school, so this was new territory for me. If my work friends weren't doing happy hour, they were at Saks, Barneys or a designer sample sale. I remember being with the group at a cashmere sample sale when my friend Rebecca picked up a $1,000 sweater that was slashed down to $400 and threw three of them onto the register.

"You should totally get one. These are amazing for travel. You can never have enough," she said while running back to the rack for more.

I remember looking down at my pink clear plastic Hermes knock-off bag and saying "Oh, I already have one."

Years later, as a self-made millionaire, I've still *never* bought a $400 sweater, to this day. (Okay, I have – but it was on sale *from* $400.)

That isn't the only way the young and foolish act young and foolish when they start feeling successful: Some of my colleagues were rolling $100 bills to snort coke off the porcelain toilet seat. Now, I love practicality just a much as the next girl, but a toilet seat? Why not use a $50 bill and use your savings to buy a mirror? Don't do this.

Any of it.

RULE #11: STOP BEING POOR

It is a mentality, not a number in a bank account. It's working hard, but also working smarter. It's investing in your future before spending money you don't have. Oh, and if a vig is getting paid, make sure it's getting paid to you.

Nothing for nothing, be careful with those credit cards because they're as bad as the shylocks back in the neighborhood. No, they won't break your kneecaps, but they will make your credit rating walk with a limp for the rest of your life.

We didn't *just* shop. It was a sport, a thrill, we were young, broke-*ish* and in the city. All of the sales women in the office recreated a sorority-like friendship and at lunch time would go into the kitchen and gossip about every person in the office: It was called by the larger office "The Alligator Pit." And my girlfriends would sit in the kitchen, pick *subject du jour* and chew their heads off. I'm not proud of this, but it was entertaining and (mostly) innocent.

I knew better, it's not like I had an excuse. My parents had instilled in me *Omertà:* a code of silence. Or, if you will, the art of keeping your mouth shut. More on that later – it's a big one.

So, I was 23, I liked my job, I was good at it. I also needed to expand; the thought of wasting my *joie de vivre* doing phone sales forever made me cringe. Besides, how could I go from boiler room to showbiz? What can I say, I'm a dreamer, I'd sit in that chaotic office with my headset on and drift off: I'd be finishing up on stage, gather my belongings, and escape with my husband and fellow comedians to a cozy bar with a fireplace where we'd have deliciously nuanced conversations over a cocktail in a luxurious piece of crystal stemware. And then I'd hear: "ELYSE! Keep smiling and dialing!" Ugh, I had to get out of here.

So, I knew I needed a staged approach (no pun intended), and I could see that the future of the publishing industry was on the web. I was obsessively reading blogs and thinking: *Companies that buy print ads need to be buying ads where the eyeballs are and, newsflash, that's no longer in print.*

Something different needed to happen. While there are a lot of advantages to being completely normal, there are advantages to being a little eccentric: Like being comfortable when creating something different. If you ask any of my closest people, they'll say "Elyse? She's always in production. Writing, performing, coding websites, renovating houses." And that'd be perfectly accurate, I've always had side creations going, or hustles, hobbies, subcontracts, artistic expressions — whatever we're calling it these days. I'm a compulsive maker, if I'm not creating things, I'm atrociously depressed.

And I mean atrocious.

These days, I spend any free time writing and performing. I don't draw hearts anymore unless they're on lunch love notes to my daughters; I still do occasionally paint. My philosophy on all things hobbies and passions is this: How are we supposed to know what we like if we don't try anything?

RULE #12: GET ON THE BUS

Another Nonni-ism I've heard my entire life. She doesn't literally mean step onto a bus, but: always try new pastimes, places, opportunities, because if we don't ... we'll never discover who we are.

Particularly in Manhattan, the variety of continuing education class options available was just mesmerizing to me. *All I have to do is pay and I can unlock forever classes?* My family always encouraged me to try everything so, here's an exhaustive list of my favorite classes I took throughout my 20s:
- Watercolor painting
- Acrylic painting
- Acrylic nude model painting
- Upholstery class*
- Interior design
- Photoshop
- Improv
- Stand-up comedy

---

* We made ottomans - I dragged my ex-husband with me. He's a mensch.

- Architecture
- Elocution lessons*
- Stage acting
- Commercial Voice Over
- Animation Voice Over

...Not cooking. I never took a cooking class, I received this innate gift from my Mother. Thanks Mom. (You see what I did there, I just told you I'm a great cook without telling you. I'm a divorced woman, you never know what single man is reading this right now. Two moves ahead. Anyway...)

In addition to all those classes I was taking, I taught myself how to code and I built websites on the side, so I took my killer boiler room-honed sales skills and applied them to these traditional publishing firms. Based on my hunch that digital media was becoming a thing, I got myself into traditional publishing houses for interviews where I convinced them they needed a head of digital ad sales, (a job I created and pitched) because this was where the future money was coming from. And they hired me

Like clockwork: I cobbled together small teams, we built-up web brands and then closed advertising deals all day long and made shitloads of money for the company and myself. I eventually started managing

---

* Ok, not really a favorite, but worth mentioning.

sales people, which wasn't nearly as fun but I always carried my own bag. I needed a little taste, needed to keep some skin in the game.

Rule# 13: Keep a Little Taste for Yourself

You want to stay motivated? Feel like you're still in the game? Carry your own bag, hold a bit back, keep your foot in the door, keep a little scarole for yourself. Which is maybe a scrappy way of also saying: don't solely rely on others.

Those classes did everything from nourishing me to inspiring me to saving me. It gave me a chance to express myself and cope with whatever I was going through.

The beauty of this was that some of my hobbies *did* become hustles. Some of those hustles turned into small businesses, even if that's not what it felt like at the time. I was just doing what I do. And so, in my twenties, here are all the companies I've had on the side:

- Beauty blog (2007)

- Cryptocurrency website (2016-18)
- Three different food blogs (2009-2014)
- Greeting card subscription start-up (2014-2015)
- Commercial voiceover artist* (2017-present)
- Stand-up comedian & podcast host (2017-present).

When I was on Wall Street, an unconventional part of my job was to host a TV show: *We needed content - don't ask.* Anyway, I was very green and on-air interviewing founders and CEOs of tech start-ups and at the end of each interview, I'd ask the CEOs to give the world a piece of advice.

Almost all of these entrepreneurs said something similar: A true entrepreneur starts hundreds of ventures but the most successful ones know when to fold them. Don't ever quit, because oftentimes, it's the 101st company that hits. *And that's another rule worth knowing:*

---

* Which is very satisfying for someone being teased about her voice growing up.

Rule #14: Keep Going

Never stop the hustle, never be ashamed to stop, pivot, scrap it and start something new. Life is a journey. As we say in show business: you'll never make it if you quit.

This is probably the appropriate time to officially tell you that I'm a professional comedian. A stand-up comedian. Every mother's worst nightmare. *Sorry Mom.*

Here's the deal: Life (if you're lucky) should be long, did you think you were just going to have one career? Maybe? Maybe that's how some of the best CEOs were made, by slow and steady wins the race. Or Maybe not? If you're anything like me, successful in business has its highs, *and health insurance,* but bores to tears. Or more importantly, I felt alone in my career... in motherhood... as a working mom. I wished that when I was feeling so alone, I could've gone to a comedy club, or a theater, to see someone on stage that reminded me of myself. *A tired, seasonally-chubby working mom, someone who didn't fit in with the corporate world.* I just wanted someone to take me out of my own head for a few minutes. Someone I could relate to, connect and laugh with. After all, I did have my life-long dream of being in show business.

So, and life is like this, an accident turned into a hobby that turned into a hustle and then something much, much more. And yes, I did this all alongside my corporate career. People ask, how did you have the time to hone the craft? Well, some people go to happy hour and I'd go home and work on my craft, and I still do. It's a journey people. I also don't watch television – okay, one caveat here is that I watch with my children... because I have to.

So, right. I left the corporate world to pursue stand-up comedy and now I'm a professional stand-up comedian. My corporate background is not exactly your typical stand-up comic's career journey, but it worked.

I'm just a regular New York City girl seizing the everyday and living life without limits. If you're not doing this, try it. *Come on... You know you wanna....*

It wasn't easy leaving the comforts (*and stock options*) of big corporate America and into the uncertain, insecure world of comedy. But I had to. I had a calling.

Cover Your Tush...
and Get Your Hand Off Mine

If you're part of a crew, nobody ever tells you that they're going to kill you, it doesn't happen that way. There weren't any arguments or curses like in the movies. See, your murderers come with smiles, they come as your friends, the people who've cared for you all of your life. And they always seem to come at a time that you're at your weakest and most in need of their help.

-Henry Hill

I left the job at the British publishing house for a major international news organization that was eventually acquired by an even larger international news organization. This was a different world from the bulls on the ad sales floor. No hand-depositing my paychecks at the new job. I had five rounds of interviews and, once hired, scheduled meetings with my "HR guidance counselor" to answer any questions about the job, the company and guide me to success. It all *felt* very safe and secure.

And they wanted me to feel that way. Companies today love to use the phrase "safe space." The larger the company, the larger the HR organization, the more bodies they have running around telling employees, particularly new hires, this is a safe space by saying things like, "Come talk to us whenever you feel the need."

There is a sensible, profitable reason companies are obsessed with all this – it makes employees more comfortable and therefore more productive. But remember that underworld? The *unspoken* rules no one talks about? Corporations are going to Cover. Their. Own. Asses.

I'd only been at the new job for four weeks when my boss David and I were wrapping up a closed-door meeting. We were chatting as people filed out, and I mentioned my upcoming weekend plans to go to the Hamptons with some friends. He got up, closed the door "Is there any room for one more?" he sarcastically smirked.

There I was, 24, newly employed, so I said, "I'm not driving but I guess I could ask."

What the hell was I supposed to do? This wasn't one of the conversations that my HR Counselor told me I'd be having with my older male boss. *Was I supposed to include him in any social affairs I mentioned? That can't be right?*

"I'm just kidding." He said, "I can't come, I'm meeting my girlfriend's parents on Saturday."

"Awesome." I said and got up, headed towards the door and thought, *Awesome? That's the best you could come up with Elyse?* As one foot stepped out into the navy-blue carpeted hallway, he quickly called: "Elyse – one more thing."

"What's up?" I said.

"You know during our interviews, I couldn't decide if I wanted to hire you or date you." He said with a laugh.

I did one of those tight closed-lipped smiles and stepped fully out of the office and closed the door.

RULE #15: **Y**OU **A**RE **N**EVER **S**AFE

Another Nonni-ism and a touch unnerving. You're never safe. From the trolls on Staten Island to creepy Dave and his revolting attempts at sexual harassment... As I started to move along in my career, it actually seemed like almost everyone was proving her right.

The next few months were almost unbearable. Dave would regularly take the team out for lunch and, as our group walked through the big marble lobby, past the security desk, and onto the revolving doors, he always made sure to ask me some unnecessary work-related questions which put everyone ahead of us, while we brought up the rear. As everyone shuffled through the doors, I would go last, him directly after me and he would quickly slap my ass.

My insides would freeze, but I'd keep walking. And honestly, it was like: Can you get your filthy paws off of my clearance rack Loehmann's skirts. Creep.

But I never did anything. Never said anything to him. Never told anyone. I guess because I didn't pick up on his post-hire verbal and physical advances, he became dismissive towards me when they didn't work.

Eventually, I found a new job. Which should have been the end of that hell hole. But, of course not, on my leaving day, my HR counselor asked me to come down for a quick exit interview. It started out pretty typical, with the counselor asking me how was my time here, why I was leaving, etc.

She skillfully asked these questions with a maternally disarming way about her. So, I blurted out the truth. "David touches my ass every so often. He also said he wanted to date me instead of hire me. I-can't-take-this-anymore-so… I'm leaving."

Her response was… polite. "Thank you for informing me, Elyse." Followed by a slight pause. "If I could give you a piece of advice?"

"Sure." I said nervously, suddenly starting to regret my unvarnished honestly.

"Keep this job off your resume. You should gather your things and go *now*." she snapped.

Umm...WTF? And here we go, another rule for you:

RULE # 16: THE UNSPOKEN ROLE OF HR

The stated role of an employee's assigned Human Resources Counselor is to help new and existing employees with any company concerns, individual compensation and any work-related stresses.

The unspoken role? HR is just 'air cover' for the people who run the show.

I didn't even give a fuck that she was straight up ignoring sexual harassment. That guy was dead to me in the Nonni sense of the word. I was more concerned with the "Keep this job off your resume" comment.

So, what you're saying is I spent two years at an unknown British publishing company. Then, I was hired by one of the world's largest financial publishing houses because of my iron-clad sales references from my previous manager and clients (tyvm), and YOU ARE cock-blocking me from adding this job to my resume? So all other future employers would never know I worked here? So my six months at this sexist cesspool doesn't even count? I paid the price God damn it, I want to put it on my resume.

To be honest, I should've taken them to the cleaners, but I didn't. I wasn't litigious and besides, I saw this as a test. A test not to get caught up in petty bullshit. He was a weasel, a real dogging hoe.

And no, I didn't have a hole in my resume. What I did was simply extend my time at the British company so it looked like I never worked for the sexual predator.

Anyway, I knew the Brits at the boiler room wouldn't care. First of all by this point I was dating Paul, my future-husband, whom I'd met there. If someone ever called to fact check my duration of employment they'd be too busy watching football and drinking pints to give a shit. And if anyone did question my length of employment? I would just tell them the truth.

WORK HAZING

You have to be like a lion and a fox. The fox is smart enough to recognize traps, and the lion is strong enough to scare away the wolves. Be like a lion and a fox, and no one will ever beat you.
– Carlo Gambino

Sometimes tests happen outside the office in more social settings like company outings or those dreaded "first-time-team-lunches."

I was 23, I was at a new job and my boss and colleague wanted to take me for a quick bite to eat. The problem was I was starving because I was attempting to diet myself into a junior-section pencil skirt from TJMaxx. I was also nursing a disgusting hangover from the 27 vodka and club sodas I'd "sipped" at the Gansevoort rooftop the night before.

When you're new - let alone low on the totem pole, you don't get to have an opinion on where to lunch if not asked! You can't say *"Yeh that's a no from me, Dawg."*

The boss was fixated on going for pizza, so when he said "Pizza at 12:30p?"

I responded with, "Great. Just what I was in the mood for." Meanwhile, I thought: *Ugh. 1. I can't eat anything solid or I'll have to unzip the side zipper 2. If I do eat, it needs to be in private because diet + hangover = animal style eating.*

So, there we were at the pizzeria and something awful happened: I spotted huge, caveman-sized corners of Grandma pie, *you know the kind where it's just a little bit burnt?* Well, just as my primitive urges were about to take over, my eyes darted through the foggy pizza glass case and I saw its naughty cousin: A Grandma penne vodka slice. Another burnt corner slice. The size? Just shy of a marble notebook and it was topped with globs of penne macaroni smothered in a delectable vodka sauce and dotted with sweet baby peas that looked like little jade pearls. It actually spoke to me, whispering, *If you don't eat me I will lodge the memory of myself in your hippocampus and I will haunt you for the rest of your hungry life.*

The boss abruptly interrupted my mid-pizza fantasy and said: "Elyse? What are you going to have?"

"That one." I shyly pointed. Great. Now I look like some underfed peasant ordering the largest slice in the joint.

"You want that slice? That's like three slices in one? It's huge. You sure?"

"Yep! I'm doing this new diet - mixing lunch and dinner thing. So ya know... pizza and macaroni sounds right on the money," *Lies. All lies.*

This was a test. This was a test in class. I was only a 23 year old newbie but everyone knows, if you go out to eat with work, you eat a salad. MAYBE a soup (*minus the slurp*), but a salad is what civilized employees eat because it requires the fork, perhaps the knife to hack down the pieces of romaine into small dainty bites.

What did I know about tests? How did I know anyone was "testing me" through my meal selection. But they were.

Rule # 17: They Will Test You

Work hazing happens. It happens everywhere. Companies never really stop testing the new kids, even if they never admit it. Don't take it personally.

Later on in my career, I'd moved to another firm that was having company happy hour at Dave & Busters. Really? Can we ban this type of forced fun? No one wants to play skeeball with the IT guy and win 10,000 tickets. And yes, that sounds like a generous amount of tickets but then you're forced to pick prizes between an unsharpened pencil and miniature yo-yo.

This particular Dave & Busters was in Times Square, a location so crowded that the company roped off the area at the bar for our private post-arcade "fun." Sliders, wings and drinks were flowing, and as the night went on, shots. My new boss came over to me and offered me a drink. And then a shot.

I declined – both. I know too well what happens when this Staten Island girl gets a taste of tequila: Hair immediately is swept-up into a waterfall pony, thick lip liner applied and I'm begging the DJ to play Donna Summer. *Even if there's no DJ.*

That's not where you want to be, so I politely declined the shot with a nice "alcohol really isn't my thing." I felt no need to expound on the immediate flood of memories of me, circa 2001, at Limelight taking absinth shots with Amanda Lepore, Kenny Kenny and Lady Fag. *I'm not sure that I'll ever expound on that.* Anyway, I smoothed down the pleats in my tartan plaid knee-length skirt, smiled and asked if he won any pencil erasers.

The next day in the office I was first in. I saw my boss and we rode the elevator up together. He said, "Good call on not drinking, you're the first one in the office today."

I passed.

They Would Not Murder Each Other

The other Dons in the room applauded and rose to shake hands with everybody in sight and to congratulate Don Corleone and Don Tattaglia on their new friendship. It was not perhaps the warmest friendship in the world, they would not send each other Christmas gift greetings, but they would not murder each other. That was friendship enough in this world, all that was needed.

– Mario Puzo
The Godfather

Remember my Nonni's advice to her impressionable granddaughter? The words that ran: "These people are not your friends. They'll never be your friend. They'll stab you in the back in a heartbeat. Don't trust anybody. Just do your job and go home. Be happy you have a job. When I was your age I had no job, but if I did I wouldn't have any friends in the office…" That advice? Remember? Well, after hearing this on repeat for three decades, I decided, *screw this, I'm actually going to try and make a friend in the office.*

So, I was 27, on my first day of work on Wall Street, and my boss called me on the phone from his office (which was out of state) to give me some of his team rules. The one that sticks out the most was: "Whatever you do, don't talk to anybody in the office. If you want to talk to anybody, ping me and I'll formally introduce you via email."

What a strange rule. *Don't talk to people? On my first day? Am I a leper? Did Nonni call you?*

At the time, I hadn't the slightest idea why Gary was telling me this. It took only a few short weeks to realize that Gary Baby wanted to control his department from afar. *Whef. And there, I thought it was something worse.* Just some good ole' institutionalized gender misogyny. Sweet little Elyse can't talk to anyone herself, she needs her big strong boss's help. But because I was new, I obliged.

A couple of days whizzed by and I realized I had another team member in the Wall Street office other than myself; her name was Cheryl. We were the only two people, not to mention the only two women, working in our department. I didn't want to fly solo so I knew I needed to befriend Cheryl. To give you a visual of Cheryl, she could've easily stepped out of Vineyard Vines website; 5'7, freckled and fair-skinned, blonde with green eyes. She was probably five or six years my senior, but she'd never tell me her age.

I'd take baby-steps (not the desperado kind from my Staten Island childhood), and roll my chair right next to hers. "Cheryl, are you ever going to tell me your age?"

"A lady never tells..." she'd whisper back.

"Who are you, Jackie Onassis?" I hissed. "What's the big deal?"

"Age is not a piece of information I dispense."

OK, Cheryl. I'd get so furious with her. What kind of FRIEND was this? Any normal person would've gladly told me their age. We were peers, at the same level, we needed a bond – sharing your birth year would be a good start, I thought. Overtime, I realized that Cheryl liked to keep an air of mystery about her. By never fully revealing herself, no one was able to box her into a generational mindset.

Cheryl and I were from completely different worlds. Her parents were former flower children; independent bookstore owners; and my mother and father, well we were just average middle-class New York City people. Cheryl had a husband, an elementary-age daughter and lived in Park Slope, Brooklyn – *which means she's not really from Brooklyn, probably an import.* In fact, I'd later learn, she was from Marin, California. Naturally this slightly annoyed me because I knew she was likely a former member of the

Park Slope Stroller Mom Mafia, a non-violent gang of, usually blondes, who traipse around Brooklyn with their Upper Baby Vistas saying things like: "I wish these EYE-talian people would take their saint statues off the lawn; it's an eyesore for the community." And you know what happens in Park Slope? The more Stroller Mafia, the less Virgin Mary action figures I'd see.

Anywho... after a lot of polite, boundaried talk, Cheryl eventually warmed up to me. That or she realized pushing my rolling office chair out of the way wasn't an option. I gotta tell you, we had a marvelous seven-year friendship; almost like a sisterhood. I mean, I did think it was a little strange every time I suggested we sometimes get together outside of work for a girl's night out rendezvous; or more boring, get our kids together for a playdate and she'd politely *and swiftly* say, "No, thank you."

Rule #18: These People? They Are Not Your Friends

Your colleagues probably like you well enough but with fussy bosses and careers to take care of, that's where their loyalties lie.

Okay, maybe the relationship wasn't that marvelous, but who cares? It's probably a California-thing to keep people at an arm's length distance.

And let's be serious, it wasn't that she didn't *like* me; after all we spent fifty-plus hours a week together. She was the first person I saw in the morning besides my husband and my daughters. If we were traveling, sometimes she *was* really the first person that I'd see in the morning. We bonded over both coming from publishing backgrounds, I was definitely more of the aggressor; she was definitely more of the go-with-the-flow type.

I finally had a work bestie - just like in the movies. I loved it. She was the first one that knew I was pregnant... before my husband. It's not that I blabbed, she called it when, one fateful morning, I showed up at my desk at 8am devouring a bag of Cool Ranch Doritos, you know, in that casual coffee and Doritos breakfast sort of way.

"You're so pregnant. OMG."

"Absolutely not." I said as the crumbs dropped into my cleavage

"Just take a test..."

"Whatever." I said, finishing my preliminary breakfast bag and opened another.

Cheryl wound up being right and a few short months later, she was at my baby shower with my family and friends. By-the-by, I still didn't know how old she was.

When Nonni spotted the only natural-blonde in the room, she remarked, "Who's the blonde and why is she here?"

My mother, probably still recalling the days of calling up randos for playdates who would *not* pelt her eldest child with rocks, chimed in, "Ma, stop. She's Elyse's girlfriend from work."

Nonni was nothing if not insistent. "Denise, co-workers aren't your friends. She'll stab her in the back."

"TIME FOR CAKE EVERYONE!"

Cheryl had an extraordinary time. Everyone loved her, especially my British then-mother-in-law. They chatted the entire party.

When I was pregnant with my second daughter it was the same again. I strolled into work armed with the Doritos and Cheryl said, "Time for another test." We, well I, shared everything – probably too much with her. When I bought my apartment, I shared the painstaking renovation details, then my interior design plans. She was there for me when my father passed away (no flowers at the wake from her, but I forgave her; she doesn't know – you know, not Italian.). I even made her swear to secrecy when I bought a small vacation home in Pennsylvania. My rationale? I couldn't buy a vacation home and then in good-faith ask for a raise, so that acquisition had to remain top secret.

It wasn't until I got fired that I realized Nonni was right. Cheryl was not my friend. I once told her that I was a very literal person and if anything, *anything*, seemed a bit strange at work, please give me a heads up. "Cheryl listen," I said, "if you ever feel that things are a little weird here in the office…at the company… Do you mind pulling me aside and telling me? Because, you know, I'm not really good at that kind of thing."

"Of course. of course," she assured me. Oh and it got weird, but I was always too busy doing the heave-ho to realize something was afoot.

After I was fired, I only saw Cheryl one time. She came and met me at a bar on the Upper East Side for a drink. She said was worried after she heard the tone of my voice on the phone. I probably was very scattered in the way I was talking – so she paid me a visit uptown. When she arrived at the bar, I wasn't even grasping the fact that I had lost my job I so dearly loved. *And, of course I wasn't grasping it.* I was the primary earner in my home, I had two tiny kids, was a top-performer; I was in complete denial.

After our bar meeting, I texted Cheryl every week for about six months straight and she never answered one text message. Actually, once she did send a biting curt response and it basically said, she was sorry for the distance and alluded something to the effect of "see you around" and "maybe one day." I waited a long time for another text, waiting for the three dots which never came.

It took over a year for me to see the reality of the situation here. She wasn't my friend. And more importantly, that my grandmother was right. I told Cheryl more than what was necessary. I never concealed my intentions with her. I was always one hundred perfect straight up Bestie-status with her and when push-came-to-shove and I was no longer at the company, to Cheryl, I was *persona non-grata*.

I think about Cheryl a lot to this day. She was by my side through so many of my life's major milestones. She was next to me when I got back together with my husband. Next to me for the birth of my first daughter all throughout my maternity leave, my return to work, not to mention my ridiculous attempts at trying to pump breastmilk in the storage closet.

She was there for the birth of my second child (*no flowers again – what's with these people?*) And, all the milestones in my continued education; pretty much all of the things that you go through with your nearest and dearest.

I wish I invested the time that I put into Cheryl with my own girlfriends from Staten Island or even with my husband. She didn't want to jeopardize her own employment, she didn't want to risk her job being a friend to me. *Asshole.*

AND INTRODUCING ELYSE

You gotta build a team that is so talented, they almost make you uncomfortable.
— Brian Chesky

When I was a kid, anytime my parents brought around a new friend, he or she would be introduced as "a friend of the family." Or, more often than not, as a new "cousin." When I was a kid my mother was always referring to "our cousins." I didn't know how this was possible because I knew how many siblings my parents had and knew all of my cousins. Still, my mother would say, "The cousins are coming over."

Being the very inquisitive child that I was, I'd naturally ask, "How are we related to them, again?"

"It's a long story. Go take the paper plates outside."

My Aunt Camille from Breezy Point, Queens was my mother's best friend in high school and her three daughters: Danielle, Michelle and Victoria were all my "cousins." At St. Brendan's in Brooklyn, they probably made one of those 80's pacts with each other: "When we get older, and have babies, we'll all be cugines. Swear on your life." I don't even know if this was a thing, but in my mind, this idea that all-our-best-friends-kids-are-cousins came from the old school.

I think I only realized we *weren't* blood relatives like last year. It doesn't really matter because they are still my cousins as far as I was concerned – we've still got that family bond. So, where I'm from, The Family brings in insiders in the form of cousins.

It's all good. You still with me?

Which is to say that introductions are important, and they need to be looked at in two different ways:

1. How new people are introduced into the circle of trust. (Gary had opinions on this.)
2. How you introduce yourself to new people you'd like to be associated with.

In the corporate world, to introduce somebody new to the team, I've learned that I have to take people under my wing if I want them to enter the circle of trust. *Or, say I wanted them to work at the company.*

I'll never forget I had an acquaintance come to me years ago when she was let go from her job in ad sales at the Associated Press. I was elsewhere in digital media when she called me freaking out, "I just lost my job. What the eff am I gonna do?"

I felt wretched for her, but I didn't know her that well; she was a friend of a friend. I also didn't know *how* she lost her job. Maybe she was underperforming, maybe she stole too many reams of printer paper, who knows? What I did know is that we were friendly and she was looking for a job in my industry. So I called up one of my friends who is the CEO of a then-very popular digital media company, and I said "Look, I have this friend, she's a killer worker. Are you hiring? You're gonna love her."

Next thing I know she got the job. *Fabulous.*

Looking back, I guess I should've thought more about the fact that she was working for the sleepy Associated Press (no offense, this was before they had a website), and this place I'd landed her was at a cutting-edge start-up located in the East Village. What the hell did I know? I was 25 and my heart was in the right place. I also know that when the shoe is on the other foot, and you're one who needs an introduction, then having someone to vouch for you makes life *a lot easier*.

What I failed to think about was that it could end in disaster – and it did. She wound up leaving that company and the guy never took my word on a rec again.

Lesson learned. What I learned was that I needed to be more careful when bringing a friend into one of my circles of trust. Again, you need this to work the other way when you are the one trying to get *inside*.

RULE #19: GET THE INTRODUCTION FIRST

Get one. Give one. Introductions are like vouches of approval, but, remember that introductions are cousins with trust.

Later, when I was 29 and working at GFP*, the company hosted an informal, once-in-a-blue-moon-invite-only series called "CEO LUNCH". The company would basically put all the employee's names in a proverbial hat and select five at random who would have a private lunch with the CEO inside his office.

This was an office for big dogs on the top floor of our skyscraper with expansive sweeping views overlooking all corners of Manhattan's Financial District. You'd walk in and see Brooklyn Bridge, Lady Libs, Freedom Tower, Central Park's Reservoir - it was really something else. So, the chosen five would sit

---

* Global Financial Powerhouse. And no, that wasn't the *actual* name of the company.

around a catered schmancy lunch with the CEO to talk about their personal and professional backgrounds, plus any ideas we had for the company. All the kind of stuff most people would shy away from. Except me. I'd die for this opportunity. It'd be a total movie opportunity, girl from a small department gets invited to have lunch, share ideas, *light camera action!* This was pretty much as showbiz as a corporate career can get I thought. What I didn't realize in my unbridled enthusiasm was that I should have had my boss introduce me to the top brass before I was invited at random.

Or, once my name was selected at random, I should've called out sick. *And of course, the flaw in this plan was that with my luck, my name wouldn't be picked again.* The advantage was that I would've dodged the awkward thing to begin with. But, I didn't. I was young. I was eager. I was hungry and I love a potential cinematic moment in the workplace.

The CEO was a regular New Yorker – your average Queens guy; his mother, Italian, his father, Irish. He graduated from a nondescript SUNY College and rose through the ranks to become the CEO of a major financial exchange. He even had a turtle farm. I mean, what CEO do you know that has such an affinity for turtles that he opens a farm? I loved everything about this guy.

Anywho, so my name gets called for this lunch series, I'm already planning my outfit.

Weeks passed and the big day arrived. I was over the moon and also five months pregnant and my neutral state was running high on hormones. I chose a classic demure look: My dark navy blue Brooks Brothers blazer with brass buttons and a pair of matching maternity slacks. When I arrived, the five of us employees had assigned seats and immediately, introductions and questions were fired. I was happily perched in my chair listening, answering, and eating. *Baby was hungry.* Most people were sheepish when it was their turn to speak, but not me, when I heard "Elyse?" in my mind, I heard, *Rolling!* I will admit, though, I was surprised when he asked me, "Where did you come from? No finance background?"

There's no code of silence that applies here, he's the *Capo Di Tutti di Capi* and he wants an answer, so I said, "I come from the media industry…"

"Okay," he said, "this is finance. How do I know what value you offer?"

"Well, I joined this company in sales to grow our digital media business. I know it's just a small business unit at the moment but with our brand IP, and my experience, we can really expand our offering, do some upgrades to our legacy tech infrastructure and this, in turn, will boost our advertising and start to be a solid revenue-generating business." I was thinking fast here but it was a honest response.

And, when round-robin style questions landed on me again, this time asking for ideas for the company's future, I gave a couple of innovative concepts for my business unit.

Much to my delight, he adored my ideas (and probably my infectious excitement just being in the room) and said, "Great. I want you to stay close to me. We don't have anybody with your skill set. Stay in touch so we can make this happen."

Killed it. I was elated.

Few weeks later, the mail delivery cart dropped off a group picture from the CEO lunch. I took it home, excitedly showed it to my husband Paul and we framed it. It was just one of those moments that I just thought, *Well, I'm on my way to making it.* It might not be showbiz but it's something.

There's just one small problem: Someone wasn't happy. And there's always someone who isn't happy, but when it's your immediate boss, it's a problem. A big one. I didn't follow the rule, I didn't go to him first for an introduction. What I hadn't done was call my boss to say I was invited to this special event. I thought it was fine, but it wasn't.

It's one of those unspoken rules of the corporate world: I either needed to have my boss introduce me, *or* I needed him to say "Of course! Enjoy!" which would have been the figurative rubber stamp of approval on my attendance.

Perhaps he was threatened by what he perceived as bucking the chain of command. Or maybe he felt snubbed, I don't know. What I do know was that I got myself in a lot of hot water. My boss was on my ass for two years after that. Even worse, I lost the opportunity of keeping in touch with the CEO because I was too scared. *Where's my chutzpah when I need it most?* But the reality is, because I was pregnant at the time, the last thing I could afford to do was sacrifice my job.

BOSSES HAVE OPINIONS

I called your f—— house five times yesterday, now, if you're going to disregard my m—— f—— phone calls, I'll blow you and that f —— house up… This is not a f—— game. My time is valuable. If I ever hear anybody else calls you and you respond within five days, I'll f—— kill you.

-John Gotti

Isn't it funny that some bosses just were born bosses?

So, meet Gary. Gary was my boss for six out of the seven years I worked at GFP. When I joined the company, he was stuck unhappily in his Upper Middle Management position at the time. *That was his major sore spot.* Gary loved when anyone in our department referred to him as *Boss, Chief, The Man-in-Charge*. Most of all, he operated on respect. Gary wanted his opinions heard – *and wanted you to ask for them.* He liked when people came to get his blessings and kiss his ring – only for you to complete the task and he would critique you on how to do it better the next time. *And "do it better" was code for "do it his way."*

Don't get me wrong here, Gary was a great guy, a real mensch, who loved Scotch, steak and civil war reenactments. He wore ordinary gray suits and ties that looked like they came from The Trump Collection at Macys. He was kind and he was very good to me while I was having my children. The best about ol' Gary Baby was that he was fiercely loyal and protected his employees as if we were in the battle of Monmouth, or better: like we were his own flesh and blood.

Gary ran all avenues of our department, including my sales and ops teams. And when there would be an underperforming person, Gary would say very funny stodgy corporate things like, "Chuck. Don't make me dust off my old sales hat and get back on the road to show you how it's done."

When I was managingI didn't really need Gary's help. I was doing it on my own, managing my own bag of business, plus managing the other sales and operations folks. But once a week Gary had a team meeting and we'd go round robin – *a corporate meeting favorite if you haven't noticed* – and give him updates about our business. Each week, I gave him a thorough download about all of our clients, and I always made sure I had prepared a couple of client conundrums I needed his opinion on.

Also, every few weeks I would request his help in strategizing on how to close a deal. Gary absolutely went balls-to-the-wall bananas for this. Like the first cannon that went off in the battlefield; he would immediately stand up at the end of the conference room and raise his arm almost salute-like, clear his throat and say, "Yes. It is my duty to help. Yes." Most times, he'd veer off and lecture the room about his own career journey and imparting his wisdom he acquired through the years. It was annoying, but I also found him rather endearing.

RULE # 20: ALWAYS RESPECT THE BOSS

Most bosses are Type-A personalities: Competitive, dominant, associate self-worth with achievements, ambitions and high-achieving goals. Many Type As like to feel *like the boss*. They want to be heard. Ask them questions. And, if they say they don't, they're lying.

Rule of caution: If you try to outshine the boss, it'll work the other way by inspiring fear and insecurity. They have to remain in control. Or at least, think they remain in control. Let them take credit *most times*.

I wasn't manipulating Gary, let me be clear. I just needed him to know I respected him and needed everyone else to see it. He appreciated that I rarely acted like a know-it-all but wanted to learn as much as I possibly could.

He ran his teams militantly and he taught me a lot about trust, loyalty and most importantly respect. Bosses need respect. Bosses have opinions and ideas. And you must let the big she/he steer the ship. Because whatever you do, you don't want Gary to turn on his own. No. That would be a career death sentence.

RESPECT THE COMMISSION

Every company has two organizational structures: The formal one is written on the charts; the other is the everyday relationship of the men and women in the organization.

-Harold Geneen

Yes, of course you have to respect the boss, first. But that's not the only figure that makes a firm or a family go. You also have to pay respect to *The Commission*: This can be a company's board of directors or, like the G7, the industrialized democratic countries that get together to discuss issues like global economic governance, international security, and energy policy.* The Italian-American mafia is made up of the heads of the families, the Capos, who come together and approve important matters – like a new boss or a new member.

---

* United States, Canada, France, Germany, Italy, Japan, and the United Kingdom, if you were curious.

But, then there is the Association, which are the peers – who are just as important as the bosses.

This is fairly easy to sort out depending on the hierarchy where you find yourself: Corporate America you generally have something like this

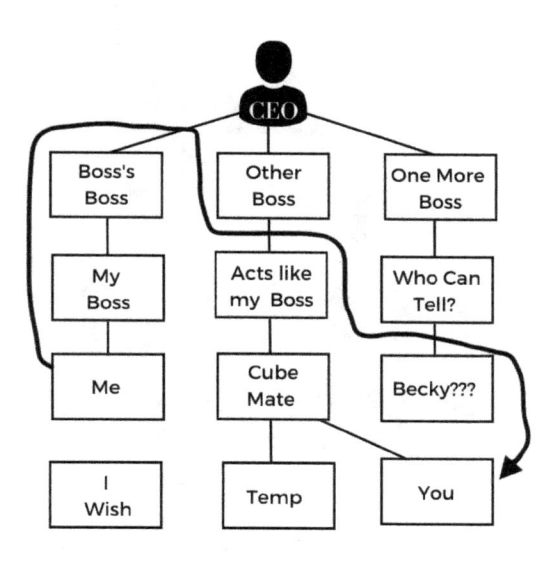

```
                    CEO
        ┌────────────┼────────────┐
   Boss's         Other        One More
    Boss           Boss          Boss
      │             │             │
     My          Acts like     Who Can
    Boss         my Boss        Tell?
      │             │             │
     Me           Cube          Becky???
                  Mate
      │             │             │
      I           Temp           You
    Wish
```

And if you were born in my neighborhood, the world looked something like this…

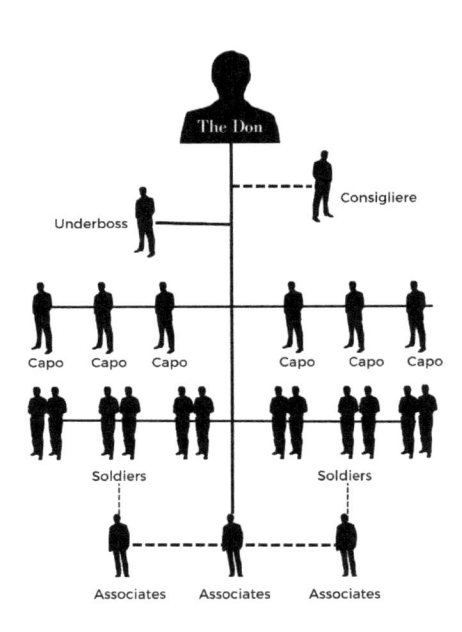

```
                    The Don
        Underboss ────┼──── Consigliere
                      │
    Capo  Capo  Capo  │  Capo  Capo  Capo
                      │
      Soldiers        │        Soldiers
                      │
   Associates   Associates   Associates
```

Basically, if you're going to do it, do it even better with food. And unless you've been living under a rock, Italians use food as not only a way to show love, thanks, acknowledge feelings; it's our universal way of paying respects. Even if we don't like you, you'll know, because all we'll serve you is a Ritz cracker. My go-to is Lancaster Pennsylvania's Kitchen Kettle village jam store. It's the gift that *never goes away*: Jams and Jam butters. Every time you open up your fridge and see the jar of apple butter sitting there, you think of me. Don't get me wrong, I do love a good Harry & David Golden Pear, or the jewel box French chocolates that is, Vosges. But, there's nothing like an edible gift with longevity.

You know who this is good for? That HR professional who hired you. I'm not saying go the great lengths to send her a jam jamboree but, how about a tasteful bottle of wine from Sherry Lehman? Actually, scratch that – liquor isn't a great gift; I mean they're working in human resources, if I worked in HR and hear all that kvetching all day – ugh... I'd have a bottle-a-day problem. How about cheese? Would a small, *and I mean petite*, wedge of gouda with a bow from Dean & DeLuca kill you? After all, he/she's the one you schmoozed on LinkedIn, complimented mid-interview and sent that barely swallowable *thank-you-for-the-interview-this-is-why-you-should-hire-me* email.

Do yourself a favor: Send the HR person a 'respect' after your first month or your first-year anniversary to tell her how much you're enjoying the work and culture of the company. *That's the commission you need to be paying respects to.*

As for me, around holiday time, I love to go big – *you know, that's very Italian...* So, around Christmas, when I'd do my baking, I make an extra ring of struffoli, put it in a plastic plate, slap some cling wrap around that puppy and place it in a visibly accessible area like on top of someone's filing cabinet with a note: "Happy Holidays!" *They'll know who it's from...*

Not only is this a delightful ethnocentric treat, I'm giving them a part of my kitchen, my home... I'm respecting not only Da Capo but I'm respecting the larger Association and by default The Commission.

Pro Tip: If you do this mid-summer, you'll have a higher chance of getting a promotion come the usual 'put-in-for-promotions" time in September.

Rule #21: Pay Respect to the Commission

In my world, we pay respect to the commission with food. For you know, certain important events:
- Huge Events: Births, deaths, etc...
- Medium Events: Job promotions, new homes, etc...
- Everyday Events: Walking to the mailbox, etc..

Two Steps Ahead

I'm only going out for a few minutes.
Anthony Strollo

Growing up, my father would tell me, "Kid. Don't share future plans wit nobody."

"Hmm...Dad? I think our neighbor Salvatore doesn't care that we're going to the movies."

"He's on a need-to-know basis. Everyone's on a need-to-know basis. Including Sally. We stay two steps ahead of all a dem."

"Mmhm."

"Listen to me..." he'd continue, taking a long drag out of his Salem Light, "If someone's making coffee, keep your eyes open. Pay attention. You know that the next place he's goin' after that is to put the milk. Then sugar. Then that little fucks going to open the draw to get a spoon. Maybe then a napkin - if he's decent."

Being two steps ahead is exhausting, but once you get it down, it kind of becomes second nature.

I WAS HIRED at a large, glamorous international magazine publishing house (the same one as *The Devil Wears Prada*) as their Digital Ad Director. What that meant was that my job was to build out the digital advertising business, make product roadmaps, implement sales strategies with the sales team and find innovative tools we could incorporate into the new online side of the business I was building.

Like I said, this place was large – so like at a lot of big organizations, there's a lot of people running around with loose job titles. I had one of these in my department; her loose job title was "Business Manager." Her name was Sloan. Sloan the Business Manager. Like her title, her actions didn't make it exactly clear what she actually *did*, and yet, she was impossible to ignore. I'd been on the job for all of about one minute and a half when she leapt out of her chair, rushed to her office door and popped her head out, "OMG.LOVEYOUALREADY. HI!. I'm Sloan. Title. Business Manager. I run digital. I'll explain. Let's grab lunch in the cafeteria and I'll tell you everything. OMG. WE'RE SO HAPPY YOU'RE HERE." *Ew. Is it too early to turn in resignation papers?*

I don't know how many Adderalls she popped that morning, or if this was her pent-up anxiety on her ride in on the Long Island Rail Road. Immediately, though, she was a problem. With an office, that mouth, that volume - literally screaming on my first day, before I even put my bags down...

Sloan, with her long brown hair, caramel highlights, zoom-white chiclet teeth, tanned skin and wrists secured with a few diamond Cartier love bracelets peeking out from the stack of her kids sleep away camp lanyard bracelets. She was a former sorority girl. She was actually Regina from *Mean Girls* before *Mean Girls*. Like a Venus fly trap, she snapped people up close to her, and then chomped them up with her painfully shrill voice and gossip. And, her length of employment? Decades.

So, as she suggested, we had lunch on my first day. She talked all about her silver Porsche truck, her shopping finds at The Americana in Great Neck and how she can't wait for her kids to grow up, so she could start snow-birding with her University of Michigan besties at The Boca Beach Club. And all I could think at our lunch in the famed cafeteria was: Who's dick is she sucking to keep this job for so long? Or more probable, who's secrets was she keeping?

Sloan was a glorified administrative assistant, one that couldn't figure out an excel formula for the life of her, but she had a cushy title and she was our very own office *tour de force*.

All of which could have been ignored except for one, tiny problem. From the years 2000-2013 or so, the digital web was still considered the red-headed stepchild of the publishing industry; no one knew what to do with *the big scary internet* cannibalizing their precious glossy magazines, so they pushed this all under "Sloan's Job." Digital was the only "cool" or "soon-to-be-cool" thing about her position. And she was threatened.

The more practical problem was that anything soon-to-be-cool, will only stay that way as long as it works. This required you to kind of be a little bit techie, a little geeky, with a healthy dose of creativity. Well, after our first lunch, Sloan would come over to me and tell me all of *her plans* for *my business*. *All of her plans.* She would tell me. And show me. And email me. And share every single vision she had for the business — all day long. It was terrifying and completely insane. *And I knew that these things weren't going to work because I'd been doing this for ten years already. She wanted to know my plans, but I knew the rule…*

Rule #22: Don't Share Your Future Plans

Keep silent, stay two moves ahead. Learn their plans, and keep people on a need-to-know basis.

Sloan's frustration and fury grew like black mold. With each passing day, she ran to our mutual boss and to explain how I wasn't being "collaborative" with her. Now, if Sloan was *MY* boss, of course I would've shared my blueprints with her. Because, as we discussed, you always wanna make your boss look good. And if I was *her* boss? I'd have reestablished Sloan's job title and description immediately.

After two weeks of sheer horror, I started to give her nuggets of what I was working on. But she stayed on a need-to-know basis for three very important reasons:

1. She was annoying and asked too many questions.
2. Parroted everything I said to anyone else that would listen.
3. Her breath stunk like Parliament Lights.

She campaigned for herself and only herself. There was no way to get her to work on my team – she wasn't the join-forces type. In many ways, we were competitive, but having that level of competition in the same company is counter-productive.* This girl made my life a living hell. Maybe that was her own personal design. Maybe it was her anxiety. It didn't matter. I left

---

* Unless you're in sales, then it's game on.

after six months; it wasn't worth the ulcer she was giving me.

Besides, she was a chain smoker and I was trying to quit.

A Performer Is Born

Many young men started down a false path to their true destiny. Time and fortune usually set them right.
— Mario Puzo
The Godfather

I don't know how it happened, but the first time I gave birth, I not only gave birth to my gorgeous daughter Annalise, but to the dormant performer that had been sleeping inside of me a lot longer than nine months. I mean, who am I kidding, I shouldn't have been surprised because I've always had a penchant for thespians and knew since my womb-debut I was meant for a career in show business.

Growing up back in Brooklyn and Staten Island, I'd had a real love for old movies and a big thanks to my mother for exposing me to the classics as opposed to usual 1980s kid dreck like *Looney Tunes*. Though, I did relish in a good episode of *Zoobilee Zoo* and drool over

Ben Vareen costumed as a snow leopard. My favorite movies and musicals to watch: *Gypsy*, *Funny Girl*, *Mame*, *Hello Dolly*, *Singing in The Rain*, *La Dolce Vita*, *Mary Poppins*, *The Apartment*. I could recite every line, verse – and more importantly I had gathered my fantasy dream dinner party invite list: Mama Rose, Miss Mazeppa, Mary Poppins and Auntie Mame. And I'd be remiss not to mention the music; I loved music, my mother would blast from our dining room, American Songbook jazz standards, The Rat Pack, and Cole Porter, Nat King Cole, as I grew up I fell in love with those and so many more: Sidney Bechet, Miles Davis, Bobbie Short, Glenn Miller, Enrico Caruso, Billie Holiday, Natalie Cole, Louis Armstrong, Ennio Morricone... really you should stop, put this book down and Spotify Ennio's score with Yoyo Ma called 'The Mission.'

I'd watch and listen to these films and songs, press rewind and start from the beginning.* And over time, little bits of each piece, character or chord became such a part of me that when I was in school, listening to yet another boring history lesson and my mind would drift off into a full-blown movie. Naturally, I was the star. And if I got bored or too tangled in my movie, I would stare out the window and envision my grown-up beautiful magical Manhattan life: Dressed in

---

* VCR days...

sumptuous fabrics, strolling down Park or Fifth Avenue at dusk, peering into everyone's windows, stumbling upon a small French bistro ordering a crusty baguette slathered in that good, thick French butter, wash it all down with a maraschino cherry-filled Shirley. And I'd get home to my jewel box apartment, I'd turn to my dashing husband and say, "Dahlin' just throw a mink on my back and invite the neighbors over for a party." Oh, they were the best daydreams…

And when I would get home from school, my mother would be blasting the music and the daydreaming in my head continued.

When I was a kid, if the VCR was occupied, I'd go to another TV, scramble through the hot boxed cable channels and land on a repeat episode of a stand-up comedy interview or performance by Don Rickles, Joan Rivers, and I'd be entranced. *How are they so funny? So quick? So lovable? And I'd think, maybe if I had talent, I could do that too.* That's the allure of the silver screen right? Escape and be whisked away into your own wonderful paradise.

That was the extent of it… I thought. I never imagined I'd be a performer – a professional, working performer. Maybe in my subconscious mind I was preparing myself for another life, but a reality? Never. I didn't have anyone push me. And I'm not blaming anyone *for the record*. I just thought the lives of those, on screen and on records, came from nepotism or really pushy stage moms, to which I had none of the above.

In school, I'd make people laugh, but I was never sure if they were laughing with me or *at me*. I wasn't a class clown – *gasp*. I wasn't sarcastic, either. I was just an eccentric, happy little macaroni eater who fantasized about living my future glamorous life inside a penthouse apartment on Park Avenue outfitted with tufted tasseled couches, a black baby grand piano and heavy damask floor-to-ceiling window draperies. *Totally normal, right?*

Fast forward to 19, I was in school at St. John's University, living at home and I auditioned for a spot on-air on a popular MTV show called *Total Request Live* (TRL). I found the audition on Craigslist. *Voila! My big break at last!* I went, I talked, they loved. They told me to come back the next day for a live taping. *Yay!* TRL, which was hosted by Carson Daly, was a big deal at this time. My job was to wear something quirky and give a quick outfit commentary on whatever music video was playing during the segment – about 15 seconds of air time. It was divine and after the taping, a casting producer who was standing in the studio, named Lauren Waters, pulled me aside and asked if I'd like to audition for a show called *MTV Hits*. She described it to me as six kids sitting around a host (then Vanessa Minnillo and occasionally, Quddus) discussing a music video lineup; it was a taped show with national exposure. No pay. *Sold. Sign me up.* So after class at St. John's, once a week, I'd take the bus into Times Square for our show taping. About a year in, Lauren told me there was an opening for a female VJ for TRL to work alongside Carson Daly. She said I had an infectious, likable personality – maybe a bit "too regional," but she wanted to share the opportunity with me.

Well, I was beside myself. I had to audition for this. She did caveat with, they already had someone in mind and was close to receiving an offer (the job went to LaLa, now known as LaLa Anthony). Lauren also said: the job required the person accepting to not be attending school, as it was a full-time position. Why bother to tell me? Oh well…with the practically-hired candidate plus full-time availability requirement, this was not an opinion for me. College meant too much, especially after Temple University, 9/11 and my parents divorce trauma roller coaster. I continued on doing MTV Hits for about another six months and then decided to start interning on the business side of media. My heart sank, but at the start of my twenties, my mother would remind me that "a paying, growing job, a career – is a must." Like, Ma', don't you want my name in lights too? And of course, Nonni would chime in: "Get a job at a big company. It's safe with beautiful benefits." *Ugh.*

Early on in my career, I'd go to work, do what I had to do and then, if I wasn't taking a class, I would be home with the TV on in the background various side hustles.

JUST LIKE YOU, I had my career to make a living and then there was my free time. And honestly, I'd put things like performing, acting and comedy as a possibility out of my head. Until I became a mother just shy of my 31st birthday.

With my new little family of three, my job at the time was becoming intense. After taking my three-month maternity leave, my boss informed me that a percentage of my upcoming bonus would be paid out as compensation to my replacement while on leave. For the record: this person was a *he*, and *he* was already my colleague on our team, so of course, I was perplexed by this. Because it wasn't as if they hired someone in my absence. And even if they did - why the *fuck* do I have to pay for that? The (large) bonus check my husband and I were counting on as a nest egg for our new family, and to pay our newly hired nanny, was now half the size. I didn't know it at the time, but I fell into a mild case of postpartum depression. I say mild because it was only shortly after getting back into the swing of our family's new schedule that I was madly in love with baby Annalise, and even excited at the thought of expanding our family once more.

Yet there was still a lot to deal with, and it was really too much. My career and being the primary earner, my new baby, juggling marriage and returning back to work for a company that made me feel mistreated. After about three months back on the job, I was at the Hilton on 7th Ave on a speaking panel at a digital strategy conference. After we wrapped up, a woman from the audience pulled me aside and urged me to try voice-overs.

"You got a great voice," she said, "cuts through the noise. You should try voiceovers, I used to do it years ago - and it's great fun."

I didn't even know what voice-overs were, but I was curious. I went home that evening and told my husband Paul, who thought it'd be good to have a hobby outside of work and home. So, I asked around and joined a voice-over group with famed voiceover coach, Marla Kirban. Marla, the Jewish mother I always dreamed of having, lived and worked out of her studio apartment on West 10th Street. We immediately hit it off and she told me that if I were willing to practice the craft, she'd introduce me to agents because "I had a strong voice." Marla, a woman of her word, quickly introduced me to agents at ICM, Stewart Talent and Buchwald. Then one evening Marla invited me over for a voice over jam and she said one of her good friends would be giving a group of students a lesson.

I showed up and much to my surprise it was Jane Lynch (Glee, etc.). Jane does a lot of animation voice over (who knew) and after the jam, she urged me to take an improv class to loosen up in front of the mic.

So I did.

I know what you're thinking – do people tell me to do things and I do them? No. As lame as it may sound, I felt an awakening inside of me. Besides, voiceovers and improv felt like a hell of a lot more fun than middle-aged men stealing my bonus money.

RULE# 23: K**EEP** Y**OUR** E**ARS** O**PEN** T**O** A**DVICE**

Don't take advice from just any idiot, because almost any idiot will give you all the bad advice you can handle. When it is someone you admire, or has had success, you can save yourself a lot of trial and error, and a lot more heartache, by admitting what you don't know and taking a little advice.

Now let me say that I've always had a flair for the biz, big productions, full scale dramatics. Sure I knew I'd fit right in Hollywood, but talent? I didn't know about that. I still don't even know if I have talent. I probably don't. And while I'm at it, I remember thinking, *what kinda chutzpah does one have to have to get on* *stage, like a real* Chiacchierone* *and wax poetic to a bunch of strangers?*

I enrolled at the People's Improv Theater in Gramercy Park and it took all about one class for me to be smitten with all my weird and wonderful classmates. I was the only one who had a corporate job and the only parent. Every week we'd gather in a dingy midtown loft space and with the direction of our teacher, we'd *"yes and"* and act out random, nonsensical, sketches and plays.

For the record, I was terrible at improv. It took me a good year to get the hang of it. I mean, what can I say, I came from a structured world and now I'm here in a windowless room on the floor acting out the role of a woodland creature?

I know what you're thinking: *New baby, twelve-hour work days... where did I find the time?* Well, it was only once a week at 7pm. I could've easily been at the gym or a dreadful happy hour with well drinks, but instead, I would escape into this zany world of playing make believe with other grownups. And like a drug, the more I performed, the more I loved it. Paul had his thing, he was a runner, and when he'd get back from a long run, he always had that runner's high. Something that I finally experienced myself when I started performing.

---

* Italian slang for a gossipy lady.

About a year later, I was three-months pregnant with my second daughter, and enjoying life. I was in a level three improv class and my teacher, film actor Pat McCartney, said to me "You need to do stand up."

To which I quipped, "I have nothing to talk about."

Omertà

Don't let your tongue be your worst enemy.
— John Franseze

One of those things that my father used to say when he was being dad was, "A fish with his mouth closed never gets caught." At the time I thought he was just telling me to shut up. He wasn't. Well, not entirely.

I don't know who originally said it, neither did my dad, probably because whoever was smart enough not to say it on a tapped phone. Dad, as well as our mystery sage, knew *Omertà*: a code of honor and code of silence that all men must oblige when they are sworn into the family. This includes not gossiping, not sharing business details and most important non-cooperation with outsiders when they get nosey.

When I was a kid, the worst possible thing my sisters or I could've done was not keep silent and tell others about "the family business." What went on inside the four walls of our semi-attached house or inside our slate gray Monte Carlo was absolutely private. *I see you rolling your eyes, Mom.*

I mean, what did she think that I was going to do? Be in the kitchen, overhear her talking on our cornflower blue corded wall phone while slurping her Diet Coke from a straw and hear her juicy details about why the neighbor upgraded her above-ground pool to an in-ground pool? What would I have even done with this information? I was a kid, this was the last thing I was interested in.

I don't know if it's an Italian thing or a 'my-family' thing, but if we talk about any inside-house business, outside-house, I'm basically out of the will.

My whole family was completely nuts about privacy, but then ridiculous things would be done. Like, on the same day my mother was on the phone talking about someone's inground pool, in walked my grandmother: "You know that cousin of mine? WELL, SHE'S DEAD!" It went without saying that my grandmother did not mean that her cousin was planted in the ground, but dead to *her*.

While Nonni was telling us that her cursed cousin was dead and being weirdly loud about it, Mommy would scream from the kitchen table, "Someone close the door, I don't want the neighbor hearing our business!"

I'd snap back from the living room couch, "Mom, you're the one who's yelling. And, the windows are open."

God forbid, we were out in public, at one of my family's usual haunts: Villa Monte. Not the pizzeria side, you understand, the restaurant side where we'd be squished around the table with mommy was telling everyone not to fill up on the bread while my sisters and I were sucking back Manhattan Special Espresso Soda (two beverages that should never be combined unless you want your kids to repeat the Columbus sailing marathon), when all of a sudden, the *we-just-arrived-20-minutes-ago-commotion* would settle down and the adults start talking.

Sometimes my mother would outline her position on why she couldn't stand my father that week; making solid points like how she's mortified that he keeps insisting on parking his 18-wheeler Mack tractor trailer on the block.

I'd overhear, pull my head up from my rice ball parm and yell: "Ma, Daddy's truck?"

… a comment was abruptly met with, non-verbal version of "Shh": *The Eyes*. The Mom Eyes.

You might be able to relate to this horrific unearthly deadpan death stare that mothers give their children when they want them TO. STOP. IMMEDIATELY.

My mother is the Queen of *The Eyes*.

She didn't even talk, she didn't have to. It's just all eyes, frozen mouth and clenched jaw. A look that said *"I'm going to pretend you didn't just yell in public about our private business."*

Noted, Mom. This sort of stuff went on for oh, 38 years and counting.

And it wasn't the gossipy Alligator Pit back on page 93* that made me realize *the hard way* that there was something absolutely sage about keeping silent.

AT 34 YEARS old, I had been working at a financial company for about seven years – and I was doing well – running a global business division that had tens of millions in revenue per annum, and juggling two children under three years old at home. Not bad. I was tapped to spearhead a multi-year digital transformation project in addition. It was an opportunity and I love a challenge. We were swapping out old legacy web technology and infrastructure and modernizing it for the 21st century. This sounds straightforward, but these overhauls get political, quickly. And let me tell you, the larger the companies, the more political these projects become.

For the digital transformation, we got the big guns out: hired agencies, we created task-force teams to work on projects like UX.UI, design back-end

---

* See Hobbies & Hustles. Go ahead, re-read it. Fun chapter.

architecture and set up revenue streams. I was involved in closed door meetings and vocally contributed when asked or was needed which was often, especially when it came time for the revenue meetings. I didn't need to follow *Omertà*. My job was to oversee my teams and that was my area of expertise. Now, I made a salary and in addition a bonus so I had a personal interest in keeping the revenues as high as possible; but more importantly, my team and I were merited on increasing year-over-year revenues.

There was, however, a fundamental flaw in this project. While I was leading the initiative, my boss was fired and my division was moved under a new business unit. So, I was flying solo until I got a new boss who happened to be the head of marketing. We (I) had hired a marketing design agency that knew *my* agenda – to keep the company's web portfolio sustainable for the future while modernizing it while increasing revenues. The big boss, however, wasn't concerned with the money. Of course, he wasn't. He was from marketing, he was more concerned with optics than cash. My point is: Marketing usually doesn't give a shit about revenues. They care about Pantone colors, flowery messaging and showcasing company brochureware like *'mission statements'* and *'core values'* & showcasing *'leadership teams'*… Zzz…Oh wait, were we still talking? I fell asleep for a second.

Rule # 24: Omertà: The Code of Silence

The mix of keeping quiet about the ongoings of what you see and hear; knowing the right time to speak and, most importantly, being the "wise one that holds the silent tongue" can be really powerful. I've worked in the corporate world for just about 18 years now, and I've always been pretty good about keeping tight-lipped. When I'm not, I regret it.

I was protective of the business's revenue streams and client relationships. After all, I built the majority of them and was very vocal and honest about the ongoing situation, which was: "While we need to move forward with systemic changes, if we move forward with *certain ones* (ahem…one's which my new boss was suggesting) we will lose multi-million dollars in revenue." In short, our digital transformation architecture change was going to tank the incoming revenue for the business.

I was very anxious. I didn't want to lose my job – and I would if all of the revenue went away. There I was leading (now co-leading a project) where one person valued money and the other valued a pretty shade of blue. And Pretty Shades of Blue was now my new unqualified boss?*

One fateful day I bumped into the CEO in the hallway who asked how the project was going. I couldn't hold it in anymore, I couldn't be cool, I couldn't follow the code of silence. I nervously said, "Well... I know I shouldn't say this to you, but there are revenue projections that I'm being asked to sign off on and they aren't realistic. They are almost falsified. And this is due to these changes I have to go along with. I'm concerned with the drop in profits, being audited... and I don't know, being dishonest with our clients – not being able to deliver them the same products. I just needed to tell you..."

The CEO thanked me for speaking up and scurried away.

I felt a ton of bricks lifted off my shoulders. Until the next day, when I was asked to come into the executive dining room for a meeting. I was fired.

Severance papers and not even a snack, can you imagine?

I should've kept quiet. I should've followed *Omertà* to the death, I would've still been employed, I would've still had my work family... but I caved. Lesson learned.

---

* Gotta love Corporate America: putting unqualified people in jobs, tucking them away and putting a nice bow on it.

SPREZZATURA:
THE ITALIAN ART OF LOOKING GREAT

I'd done my time in corporate America, from McDonald's making shakes to Morgan Stanley making deals and, yet, I felt awfully constrained by the uniform – not just my clothes, but how I felt I needed to conform – that a traditional job required me to wear.

-Chip Conley

When I was a kid, my parents had date night every Saturday night. One of the highlights for me, aside from having a babysitter who didn't believe in bedtimes, was the moment when my parents came down the stairs from their bedroom and I got to see their evening ensembles.

My father, 6'ft tall handsome, with his jet black salt and pepper hair, tanned ruddy skin, gold chain and swagger that would have Biggie roll over in his grave, would glide down with carpeted steps with a pair of shiny black crocodile shoes, pleated black dress pants, a dark cashmere turtleneck, a sport coat and a solid gold watch from "his uncle" who really was my Nene's (paternal grandmother) dead boyfriend. Every step he took left his lingering scent of Drakkar Noir. He'd sit on the edge of our cream silk patterned sofa, over-dramatically checking the time on his gold watch and every five minutes would yell out, "Denise!" And under his breath, "God forbid we should ever be on time."

Twenty minutes later, the upstairs bathroom door flung open to a waft – a thick cloud of smoke formed of a lethal combination of Yves Saint Laurent's Opium and Aqua Net. I'd be sitting on the carpeted floor near my father, looking up and there'd be pixie dust-like sparkles in the puff of cloud. While my mother would like to say it was sparkles from her ethereal presence, it more the combination of aerosol gas and dust from her pale blue eye shadow. My mother would emerge from the smoke like the material girl-era Madonna coming up from the stage floor. Her eyes wide open, she'd yell out a soap opera breathy line: "I'm ready!"

I'd squint and see her outfit: patent-leather seafoam green toe-cleavage stilettos, silk M.C. Hammer hot pants, a wide black elastic belt with a large oval gold clasp, gold lame blouse and shoulder-padded jacket fixed with a long diamond flower brooch. Her hair was teased, picked, rolled and spiked stiff. Her hairstyle hasn't changed since 1973, bright red with gold highlights; moussed and Aquanetted down into the shape of an egg. She left one pink foam roller in her bangs, put her hand up and would say, "Before you even say it. Roller comes out when my coat goes on."

On cue, my father would stand up, grab her Saturday night coat out of the closet, an ankle-length beaver fur, hold it up and exasperatingly say, "Now."

My mother would make a quick glance over at us, "Girls behave!" Then she'd turn to our 80 year-old babysitter, Anita, who was hunched over the kitchen table paging through the weekly supermarket circulars, "Macaroni's on the stove, Marino's ices in the freezer. Only one each!!!!"

And with that, they glided out of the house, hopped into the Monte Carlo and within fifteen minutes had flown through the Brooklyn Battery Tunnel and arrived at their go-to restaurant in Little Italy – S.P.Q.R. One of my father's brothers worked there, his wife was the coat-check girl and it was a place where everyone knew everyone's name. The food, drinks and cigarettes flowed till close.

My parents were middle-class people, they didn't have a ton of money but they wore their best stuff when they hit the town because of *Sprezzatura*. Which is basically Italian for: The art of looking great but without looking like you put in an effort to look great. Or what fashion advertisers today spend fortunes trying to emulate: *Effortless chic*. It's the *"Oh us?*

Fabulous? Oh... We just threw on an outfit and ran out the door."

...Sure you did, Mom.

I'm pretty certain if I have an early death it'd be from second hand aerosols asphyxiation.

Sprezzatura is a large part of the Italian culture that we brought over with us from the old country. Italian-Americans love tradition, and *La Bella Figura*: literally, The Beautiful Figure. LBF is a concept that started in 14th century Rome. It's hard to get more traditional than that. It's based on the code of honor; a sense of self, decency, decorum. It basically means: look good and act the part.

It's a lifestyle.

It's an all-encompassing word that Italians use to 'make a good impression,' because the last thing we want to do is make *La Brutta Figura* – a bad impression.

Italian-Americans don't talk about LBF much; because many of us are second, third and fourth generation and the concept is so just rooted in our culture that it doesn't bear repeating. However, when I was in Rome studying abroad, my sophomore year of college, *La Bella Figure* was actually taught to us in school. Some cultures instill mathematical values. Italians? We're all about the show. We love it. *I love it.*

It's worth mentioning that this is not just superficial; along with dressing well, a big part of LBF is acting with grace. Or, if you will, *a low-key flex*. Need examples? Wearing a tasteful outfit when you're out shopping, as opposed to dressing in pajamas. Or, inviting friends over and putting out a tastefully presented hearty meal and making sure no one's plate or cup is ever empty; all while enjoying the ambience of your beautiful home. And, it's also showing off your qualities, even your power, your *je ne se quois*, so people have a higher opinion of you. It's assumed that if you practice **LBF**; people will hold you in a higher regard. This to Italians, is important. And people like my parents practiced **LBF** everyday; they just didn't know it. We like to look smashing, hold court and entertaining conversations; that's just what we do.

For my parents specifically, a cardinal concept was that their daughters, *ahem moi*, conduct themselves with decorum, which meant always telling the truth. My father would say, "When I ask you a question, you answer. You tell the truth otherwise you betray the family. If your mother or me asks for needed information, our expectation is you give it to us. One more thing: family business stays with the family. Not family? Then answer truthfully and only answer what you're asked. *Capisce*?"

It stuck with me.

THE EARLY PART of my career that was spent in publishing, the dress code was much more casual that the power-dressing of Wall Street, but that doesn't mean that media companies didn't want us to have a "look." This wasn't discussed in the interview process, but unless you've been asleep at the wheel, when you go on a job interview, the recruiter and hiring manager want to make sure *your look* will fit in with the rest of the company culture.

When I was 27, I had a female boss, Carole. Like me, she started her career in traditional media, and spent many years as the head of sales at a popular health and fitness magazine. Now she was the leading sales and operations at a venture-backed ad tech start-up, where I reported into her. She was gunning to become President of the company; and at any moment, I thought she would start to lecture us on taxation laws or something equally comatosing.

Carole had a very savvy, polished and strong personality but her clothing said: Talbots, Lerners (if you can jog your memory) and a cheque skirt suits from Lord & Taylor. Round-toe pumps with a smudge heel was her footwear of choice. *Disastrous.* She had mousey brown shoulder length hair, wore metal-framed glasses probably, from Cohen's Fashion Optical. Her wardrobe screamed: "I do mortgages in a strip mall in suburban Connecticut."

On the flip side, the sales team were all senior sales people, myself included. We wore dark-colored jeans, button down shirts, and plastic glasses. For footwear, I opted for a Tods driving moccasin or a Ferragamo

Varina. And while you want to look good, never carry a designer monogrammed bag: That just screams "I don't need a raise."

A note here: I would've been much more comfortable wearing my signature style, my own garb: a velvet smoking slipper, a long-silk kimono from my collection, a loosely tied leopard neck scarf and a bag in the essence of faux Faberge egg, but hey, life's a stage. I had to dress for the culture. I digress.

So, one day, Carole pulled me aside and said "Elyse. My office. Have a personal question."

Oh God, she found my food blog, ugh. "Sure, what's up?"

"Do you mind me asking where you buy your clothes? Your outfits are very fitting for the tech we're selling; I want, no need - I need to dress 'cooler'... Any tips?"

Oh GOD! Now I'm supposed to tell this woman I buy all of my clothing at 7am when Century21 first opens or at Loehmann's when they have their end of season clearance sales? Those are my secrets! Should I make it up? Think quick! So, I said… "Well…I buy my jeans at Bloomingdale's" lie…. "my shoes – I only have a couple of pairs at Barneys" ….ew, more lies… "and my tops, exclusively at Thomas Pink, Brooks Brothers." Lie. Lie. Lie.

Carole brightened up, "Perfect! Can we shop one day after work? Actually, let me just get you a card."

She flipped open her first edition MacBook, loaded the American Express site where I saw a $12,000 bill.

"Shit. My husband said he paid this month's bill. ...Last week, I tried to shop. I bought all of this stuff... look at these prices," pointing me to the screen.

"I already gave it to my housekeeper. Wasn't the look," she said.

Meanwhile I was hung up on the $12,000. In one week? And that's how you dress? My eyes were fixated on her screen. I'd totally forgotten about the Magellan expedition she wanted me to go on, and yet I was still thinking: Isn't it enough that she had to come with me to the shittiest meeting of all time to Fidelity in Boston and now she wants to Romy-and-Michelle clothes-shop together. No. Actually she wants me to become her personal shopper. Absolutely not... Actually, on second thought. Does this job pay a commission?

Eventually I managed to say, "Carole, you know what would be so much easier and efficient for your busy schedule? My friend's sister IS a *real* personal shopper and she would love to help you."

"Done. $12K a month. No, $15K. Will that work?"

"Sure..."

Which was all well and good until I saw her the next day and she announced, "Elyse, cancel the shopper. Do you know Hannah? The intern? Well, she's also my niece (surprise!) and started shopping for me. She's on the job."

"Great," I said, doing a decent impersonation of someone with two and a half shits to give.

All I can say is two short months later Carole looked not only 15 years younger but that she was about to close a Series B round of funding.

Rule #25: Dress and Act the Part

No matter the day or age, clothes and behavior garner respect.

For me, I eventually learned how to dress the part, I added a statement necklace, and by statement: I meant a triple string of Tiffany pearls. I wore a Longchamp bag, light makeup (no lip liner) and no morning use of my beloved hot-rollers.

But the clothes garner respect. I eventually found my own clothing groove: Suit pants, a sleeveless shell and a navy Brooks blazer with gold buttons, popped collar and loafers. It was a look that said: *I'm the Don Dada*. At least in the business world.

Let me tell you, the tables reversed themselves when I got to Wall Street. I was 27, and it was my first day at work. I had a dreaded orientation which consisted of a windowless conference room filled with a projector screen and a wasteland of robotic voiced

PowerPoints going over everything from HR handbook and benefit selections.

After devouring two mini roasted turkey wraps, a bag of salt and vinegar Zapps chips and four bottles of lukewarm Fiji water; the New Hire Director instructed us to go to our desks for the last hour of the day, "make ourselves comfortable" and "explore the blue welcome gift bag" on our desk chair. Inside, was a folded-up bankers duffle and other goodies that we were expected to take advantage of: A keycard lanyard, an aluminum branded water bottle, mouse pads, a logo'd fleece vest and basic office supplies. *Just what I love to find inside a blue gift bag.*

As I looked at my new desk, and my eyes shifted over to my desk phone, I saw a small navy blue envelope from Brooks Brothers labeled "For Elyse", I opened it up and it read, "Welcome to the family! Please find a Brooks Brothers club card which offers a 20% off corporate discount along with your own personal shopper." And then a pen drawn line underneath with my shopper's name, Sarah.

Brooks Brothers had a giant store downstairs inside our office building. So, later in the week, after I started getting in the swing of things, I went to introduce myself to Sarah. I mean, I had no idea who this person was; Is she an employee of the store? My firm? Do clothing narcs exist? I'd already cleared our Century 21's career section, what more could I need? Maybe having my aunt & grandmother dress me the day I interviewed was not my finest idea; probably wearing a leopard belt fell into that category too. But you know, to me, my wardrobe screamed: I'm business but I also have a hint of dazzle.

Shopper Sarah had other ideas. She firmly shook my hand, took me on a brief (and unnecessary) store tour and explained my new company's preferred color palette: navy, black, charcoal gray & white. *Where's the leopard?* She then proceeded to take my measurements and fill a large dressing room with items; You know, one of those rooms that has the circular carpeted alterations stage in it? Next thing I knew, I had a $3,000 "discounted" bill with clothes that outfitted me as a cross between a flying nun and a court stenographer. Sarah talked like a female pimp transforming her finest hooker into a statesman: "French cuffed sleeves always need cufflinks. Start with these tasteful fabric knots. Never go without pantyhose, take these….And, lastly - don't let me see you in heels higher than two and a half to three inches," she quipped.

Wow, fun. Can't wait to ask her to go for a happy hour cocktail.

KEEP YOUR EYES OPEN AND YOU'LL FIND VERSAILLES

There are three ways of doing things around here: the right way, the wrong way, and the way that I do it.
— Robert De Niro
As Sam 'Ace' Rothstein in *Casino*

When you look like a million bucks, you'll feel two million bucks. And on Wall Street, there's a lot of bucks going around. I had a short-lived friendship with a Russian woman, Yana. She was over-the-top fabulous; her look was like if 1982-Ivanna Trump and Coco Austin* had a baby. Yana grew up in a one-bedroom apartment in Brighton Beach, Brooklyn and after making some dough in finance, she bought a two-bedroom apartment in Dumbo inside the most exclusive building in the neighborhood, One Main. She loved to tell me

---

* Ice-T's wife, go ahead, google her.

that her guest room was decorated with a theme to her favorite vacation destination, St. Barts. Still to this day I don't know what this means but I'm going to assume it was a Caribbean-themed bedroom. Not my thing – but likely akin to how my wall-to-wall leopard carpeted living room might not be your thing.

Anyway, shortly after I gave birth to my first daughter, I dragged my tired ass into the office with Cheerios stuck together on the bottom of my shoes and dried spit up stains on my Longchamp tote bag. Yana came over to my desk, slapped down her new Louis Vuitton purple patent leather handbag on my desk and in her thick Russian accent said, "Do yourself a favor. Buy decent designer bag."

I went online and tried to find the price. At the time, Louis Vuitton didn't put prices on the site, so during my lunch break, I walked over to the Soho store. It was $4,000.

Never.

As soon as I returned, I marched straight over to Yana, "$4,000!? On something that will never appreciate in value, really?"

"Yes, it will. It's *real* Louis." She laughed.

"Not when every day you overstuff it and slap it around on people's desks," I pointed out as I took a bite of my homemade PB&J sandwich.

"Life. It is meant to enjoy Elyse-bubbachka," she melodically laughed.

Exactly two weeks after that conversion, we bought a vacation home and didn't slap the deed on everyone's desk.

R‌ule # 26: Never. Ever. Tell Them How Much Money You Have

One thing I've observed about most senior executive women on The Street, is that they aren't running around with five carat diamond rings and Gucci-logo'd boots. Do you know why? Because they won't get a raise. Nothing screams "I don't need the money" like a $12,000 Birkin bag.

As I type this, I'm 38 years old. Looking back, I'm very pleased with how hard I worked because early in my career, I was a solid earner. By the time I was 26, I was managing a team of about twenty people. One of the girls on my team asked me why I bought my jeans at the Gap and she told me about this then-new brand of jeans, J.Brand. I was so embarrassed *God knows why*, that after work, I stopped off at Bloomie's and bought four pairs of these $150 jeans. The name-brand high lasted for about 6 minutes and I happily went back to wearing my Gap denim.

I mean, I *could* buy $150 jeans… but then that's $150 *less* that I would have to spend on my dream apartment – which before I make 'big' purchases, I sometimes ask myself: *what will be more valuable in 30 years…*

I mentioned earlier that I'd been looking for the right apartment for 34 years, and sometimes you just know, like when I found what would become my Sanctum Santorum aka eventual Love Bunny Cottage, my pre-war apartment off 5th avenue in Manhattan's Upper East Side. When I discovered it, it was a real diamond in the rough; nothing to look at and the place stunk like cigarettes and cats, but somehow I just knew.

RULE # 27: USE YOUR IMAGINATION

It's a gift after all. And there is a huge value, personally and financially, in seeing value where others can't. Following the herd can get expensive – and boring.

I found this apartment in the drop dead doldrums of winter - the absolute perfect time to apartment hunt in Manhattan because most are frantic with the holidays, hosting and everybody else are busy with apres ski.

My realtor...actually, let me erase that, because I didn't have a realtor. The real estate-listing agent, Jared, prepped me as he opened the apartment door. "This place is a shithole. Ready?"

"Shitholes are where I find treasures, can we just open the door?" I pressed. As I pushed my way into the small closetless foyer, I held my nose and started to walk through the uninhabitable apartment without saying a word.

Walking the creaky floor boards, it was obvious the joint hadn't been renovated since the early 1950s. The ceiling was crumbling down, everything from the walls to window frames to metal gates on the windows were destroyed – barely intact and covered in amber-colored cigarette smoke stains. The apartment was vacant and it looked as if someone was illegally squatting. When I opened one of the closet doors, I found a pair of tube socks stuffed inside a grimy plastic bag that read *Nobody Beats The Wiz*. (Remember that store?)

We made our way around the 1,000 square foot space and Jared, thinking he'd made his point, asked, "Can we leave now?" and he swung open the front door, turned to look back at me with a furious glaze that basically said *I hate you because I'm never going to get these five minutes of my life back.* I rolled my eyes and followed him out of the apartment. Out in the hall he didn't even bother to lock the door. And that was that.

It was a terrific building, you understand. Together we got into the burled wood elevator, he pressed the shiny brass lobby button. As we exited, I followed Jared past the white-gloved doorman onto the sidewalk, where he said: "Can I give you a piece of advice? Move to Jersey. Move to Westchester. Just go. Cut the cord. There's nothing in your price range and that's why you can't get a broker. No one's representing sub $1M buyers in Manhattan."

I stood there, waited for him to finish and when he came up for air, I lowered my oversized jet black sunglasses and said: "We'll take it. Full asking price. I'll have my lawyer email you shortly." And just like that, I was headed towards the subway back to my office downtown.

As I sat on the subway, I thought, there *was* an apartment in my price range, a great one. More than that, The One. Lucky for me, I had just the eyes and the dream to see it. My then-husband and I spent one year renovating and restoring the apartment to its pre-war glory while, of course, adding its signature Elyse DeLucci touch.

NIGHTGOWNS & SCREAMING

On a daily basis I consume enough drugs to sedate Manhattan, Long Island, and Queens for a month.
— Jordan Belfort

I can't understand why people do drugs. I mean, would you do them if you were me? My shrink once mentioned my high-functioning ADD and I have a laundry list full of self-diagnosis: Neuroticism, general anxiety, fickle, hypochondria, a splash of OCD – and not to mention that I deeply identify with Second Hand Rose (*a 1965 score sang by one of my idols, Barbra Joan Streisand*). Besides, I'm much too piggish when it comes to spending my money on drugs not food. I'd rather use my hard-earned money for a corned beef sliced thin on rye, a bowl of matzo ball soup, square knish (*never a kashi*) and wash it all down with a few cans of Diet Dr. Brown's Black Cherry. And, for the grand finale: A slice of rich, creamy cheesecake bigger than my head. Even if I yearned To do illicit substances, with my eating habits, I couldn't afford it.

Anywho, remember the boiler room, my very first job? It just so happens that in addition to fugazi magazines, my coworkers were snorting lines of blow off the toilet seats with rolled $100 bills. *Not exactly the romantic work environment I envisioned.* And so, I never partook.

Well, this isn't really a tell-all, but there was one time when I was living in Rome during college. My roomie, Kary, and I popped over to Amsterdam for the weekend – she was dying to go to the Cannabis Cup, the international weed festival. Being the sucker that I am for an impromptu adventure, and not knowing what cannabis was, I happily took the trip.

So, there we were in Amsterdam, land of *de klompenboer* or commonly known as the wooden clog. We waited in a long line to get inside the Melkweg, a popular convention hall that was hosting the event. And as always, when I'm in new surroundings, I get nervous and my tick is that I become ravenously starving. *No surprise there.* Kary was like, "Really, Elyse? You need to eat right now? We just got here," and she fisted over a handful of my favorite, Raisinets. Exactly one hour later, I left Melkweg and graffiti'd dragons on metal garage doors started chasing me down the windy bicycle-filled streets of Amsterdam. Kary gave me magic mushrooms. Kary, it's been 19 years and I'm still mad at you for that.

When I was 35, the analysts on my floor would go to happy hour a few times a week and invite me to join in. Why not? I had the two kids, I was living nearby in Battery Park, my then-husband was desperate for me to get a hobby, so what's the big deal to pop over to Stone Street for a couple of cheeky ones, eh' mate?

One rainy night, we stayed at Stone Street until the bars shuttered and we all made the pilgrimage into the deep, dark windy cobblestone streets of the Financial District and arrived at, upon entering: a dive bar.

A *bikini* dive bar, to be precise. This was a thin narrow place and the bartenders looked like aging Hawaiian tropic models in iridescent polyester string bikinis while they served well-drinks and cans of beer. I don't get it; this was only in 2017. Why was this dive bar still in existence with bikini bartenders? Haven't we progressed beyond this by now? I mean, can you imagine if the roles were reversed and some old broad opened a bar where the men were in their skivvies making us cosmos and espresso martinis? It'd be like: *Ew. Put it away. Go back to Chippendales circa 1987.* I have absolutely no idea if this place is even still around.

Regardless, it was on the night that tiny mystery Ziplock bags of powder were being passed around. Yes, I may have thought Kary's mushrooms were Raisinets, but I knew cocaine when I saw it.

Rule # 28: Don't Do Drugs

Not the unprescribed sort. I don't know about you but aren't we all getting a little too old for this? If you got to get your kicks somewhere why not swap out the powders and pills for fun drugs like: TransFats. Me personally? I prefer life's version of cocaine: French fries, nightgown sex and screaming.

If you're rolling your eyes reading this part, do it at your own peril because your reputation, professional relationships with clients, boss, and co-workers– along with your real relationships – are in the balance. And you do *not* want to confuse the last two, which is easy to do if you're cross-eyed on black market pharmaceuticals.

It's even harder when you work on Wall Street or some other male-dominated industry where it's work husband central: Just a bunch of husbands wearing Patagonia vests and Ferragamo loafers scurrying around. *Just sayin'.*

Rule #29: No One Respects a Hoe

There is nothing wrong with a little harmless flirting, I met my husband at work. But you need to keep your professional and real relationships straight.

Because…

REPUTATION IS EVERYTHING

It takes 20 years to build a reputation and five minutes to ruin it. If you think about that, you'll do things differently.

— Warren Buffett

Did your family put the fear of God into you about "ruining your reputation"? I know mine did. They would always say to us, "Your reputation is everything." They talked about it on a scale that would make any reasonably well-adjusted person thoroughly paranoid. "People will watch your every move. Your good moves and the bad moves. Don't run with the wrong crowds. Don't do anything that you're going to regret." They told me this almost as if every day of my waking existence was going to get tallied up on a permanent reputation record. They instilled in me that my character is a treasure, and it had to be pristine.

Of course, I made mistakes: like the time I thought self-tanning lotion was a good idea until the inside of my Thomas Pink white collared shirt told me otherwise. Or the time I took my "never-take-no-for-an-answer" mentality and applied that to a toxic romantic relationship. *And by-the-by, after a blowout argument with this sloth of a boyfriend, I showed up to a very-soon-to-be-ex-boyfriend's house only to find his slovenly, fat ass black-out drunk along with another girl, their naked bodies interlocked like human Jenga. What a horror*

I'm probably still making other like mistakes, even now, like by becoming a viral TikTok virtuoso during the pandemic. *I probably shouldn't have broadcasted everything.* But, in business, the biggest lesson I learned about reputation was when I had a boss leave. It was indirect because I didn't do anything to my name, *per se*, but it left me and my team without cover. We were exposed to the judgment of others who didn't necessarily want me to succeed.

I WAS WORKING at GFP, which likes people to look and think a certain way. My department, however, was similar to the misfits clique in school; we were tech people from all over the world who all had very specific expertise and skill set; some hired from the outside, some adopted from other departments; but we worked as a team, worked hard, did a good job and delivered solid results.

Our boss, Gary, oversaw our group of quirky, lovable oddballs. As far as he would share, top brass were always pleased with us. *Ahh, the snug existence of being sheltered from storms.* Not only were we sheltered, we didn't even know storms existed. It was sheer bliss, even if we had to deal with our sometimes pain in the ass, Military Captain, Gary. He dealt with *them*, the rest of the higher ups at GFP who thought we were a little off the spreadsheet for their tastes. And when he left, the house crumbled. The roof blew off along with the sides, front and the back. Really, and this is the God's honest truth, a lot of genuinely good corporate employees were affected. Gary was brutally retired after over 25 years of service because bigger sharks swam in the waters and assumed Gary's job should be eliminated. I was sad when he left. He was needed. He ran his teams well and he provided crucial air-cover from the elements.

And as you know, once the brass ring gets to come inside the house and see who was on the team and they made their own judgments. When the parent leaves the house, the kids relax and have fun for a short while, but then everyone looks around and sort of like: *Well, what the f*** happens now?*

RULE #30: REPUTATION IS EVERYTHING

Your reputation can intimidate people. It can win battles and it can also be a deciding factor in losing battles. So if there's one thing that you can ever really use from this book, keep your reputation absolutely pristine and you'll give no one anything to talk about.

So, I stepped up. I was told to take over his responsibilities and I knew how to do his job. And more importantly, I was reliable because every year since being hired, I outperformed my yearly goals, never giving any cause for concern. But once our reputation defender was gone, I was on my own. And it let me tell you, the waters were treacherous and nerve-racking: I was doing my job in the trenches, I was managing people, plus juggling operations, revenues plus profit & loss statements. To top it off, I had a new set of eyes on me. I was called into a series of meetings with other divisions and executives, where they asked a lot of questions on the components of my job, how I do my job, what I would want my dream job to be and the always-ominous, *where do I see myself within the company in five years?*

I was so enmeshed with the organization, my work, my full house at home – literally – my guard was down and I failed to realize that they were sizing me up (or setting me up to fail). They were asking me questions and through my answers – which some were unconventional for a financial exchange – maybe I was inadvertently ruining my own reputation.

Generally speaking, I don't believe that we should care about what others think about us, but, at work, *we have to care*. Corporations are insular universes. Mini worlds that need structure. If the head of that structure exits stage left, you're left exposed.

So, taking pride in your work, hitting goals, and making sure your hair is washed is part of the day to day, but even more essential is tending to our reputation. A wise colleague once told me: If we don't care for our reputation, others will decide for us. Reputation is power.

SLICE THE GARLIC THIN

I usually lump organized religion, organized labor, and organized crime together. The Mafia gets points for having the best restaurants.

— Dave Beard

Remember that terrific scene in Goodfellas when Big Paulie slices the garlic? The crew is in prison, but they bribed the guards so they are living in this big dorm (separate from the other inmates) wearing unconventional prison garb in the form of terry cloth robes and Adidas tracksuits? Remember how they were smoking cigars, drinking wine and cooking a family dinner? Antipasto, pasta, meatballs, lobsters, *you know, totally normal jail food?* Well, the point is that Big Paulie, is in the kitchen (of their prison chateaux) and he is using a razor blade (again, in prison) to delicately slice a clove of garlic to thin, tissue-like perfection because when incarcerated, he explains, dinner was always a big thing.

Remember that scene? If not, put this book down right now and go YouTube it.

...Back?

So, you might be wondering why am I talking about garlic in this book? Well, we love food, right? And if you're from any kind of culture like me, it's an integral part of our our upbringing and lives. But it's really the central part of almost everything: from organized crime families to corporate organizations. Why? Because food is accessible, allows us to feel luxurious and brings people together. You don't need to go to Sing Sing to know the difference between a good meeting and a bad meeting: *A tray of sandwiches and a cookie platter.*

You know what's the difference between nice colleagues and shitty colleagues? The work friends that invite you out to grab a slice on a lunch break.

What I love about Big Garlic-Slicing-Paulie is that he's the biggest guy in the organization, and he's doing the smallest task. And he's *doing it right.*

RULE #31: SLICE THE GARLIC THIN

The biggest boss, with the biggest stature, knows that no job is too small. That's a huge rule of the corporate world when you are, or want to be, the boss: Show your willingness to get right into the trenches with everyone else and do the dirty work.

It always reminds me of Gary – from the last chapter... remember? My Scotch and Civil War reenacting boss? Well, when he told my sales team, "Don't make me grab my bag and sales hat and go out there selling." He wanted to show that he could still be one of us; that he *was* one of us.

Not to mention, Paulie's precision garlic slicing also shows us that slow and steady wins the race. Take time, calculate, know your moves, because if you want to get ahead, go slow and perfection will (*hopefully*) ensue. We all know that guy that just slapped together the presentation the night before and what did he do? Fail.

So, I Tried Standup

All our dreams can come true, if we have the courage to pursue them.
—Walt Disney

Just before Gary was fired, he got me into an Executive Education program at University of Pennsylvania's Wharton School to study Leadership and Managerial Economics. *Titillating.* I don't if he knew he was going to be leaving and my admission was his attempt to prepare me to take his job. But more likely was that I begged to be in the program with such gusto that he just folded.

I was 32, the division I worked for changed overarching business units, Gary was gone, and I became responsible for every aspect of the business, which included managing people from sales to strategy to reporting in numbers to the CFO. Yet, as my pregnancy with my youngest daughter progressed, my job became unbearable, or rather people I was working for made it completely insufferable. Work, school and home, but it was my mental health that took a real plummet. I was with-child and I couldn't cope with the corporate politics; gaslighting, mental gymnastics, large – *and many times redundant* – responsibilities and the thought looming like a black death cloud: *Are they going to make me pay for my maternity leave – AGAIN?*

I would come home from work and cry to Paul. And while he was a very good listener, he couldn't understand why I couldn't just brush it off, leave the office at the office. But I became obsessed; and isn't it funny what good old gaslighting does to you?* That's the danger of being a part of, or managing, a unique small business inside a big company: Once organizational structure changes, the lid is off the pot and next thing you know you have non-chefs in the kitchen and all the food spoils.

Anyway, this went on for a good two years and Paul and I were fighting; the job, babies – about everything any couple with two children living in a small space could argue about, then money, renovations to the apartment, the loss of my father, but overall it was primarily due to my job. It got so bad that I was constantly sending Paul a flood of panicky mid-day texts – it was too much. Our sex life went down the

---

* By definition, gaslighting is psychological manipulation to the point of questioning one's sanity.

drain, pretty much forever. He was suggesting I quit my job and we move away. What also didn't help was that my shrink prescribed me heavy sedation medication so I can deal with the gaslighting at work.

Where I really fucked up was, even though the bright orange label on the label said: *Caution Do Not Drink*. I drank. (Not while pregnant!) When I'd attend work functions I felt I couldn't say no to anything – not even a measly drink. I was too scared, so I'd have a cocktail to stay in the cut, in the clusters of happy hour conversations. The combination of the sedative and alcohol relieved every stressor I was mentally and physically feeling. But it was short lived because I'd come home and I would turn. I would turn into a sobbing, anxious, needy, monster. I couldn't turn off the work-talk faucet. I was crazed. I missed so many milestones with my babies… I was missing the whole point of life.

He'd plead with me to quit because it wasn't working. I relentlessly shoot back, "I have work under control, revenue is at record highs, there are growing pains but I got this" And then one night, with both babies asleep, the arguing got so bad, so out of control, that at 11pm I changed out of my nightgown and ran out of the house.

And I knew exactly where I was going: To my first open mic at the People's Improv Theater.

The PIT had a Wednesday late night open mic at 11:30 pm, on the 3rd floor of the theater – which was an attic space. Literally. A triangle shaped attic space with matted maroon carpeting, a mic stand and ten cheap black folding chairs for comedians and any onlookers. My improv teacher had told me, "One night you should swing by and jump on the mic." To which I thought, *people with two babies and a nine to five, don't usually "jump on the mic" at midnight.* But, I did.

RULE #32: YOU GOTTA LAUGH

It beats crying.

Arriving in the room a few minutes before 11:30 pm, I looked around at the comedians with little notebooks, fidgeting with small tripods for their phone to tape their set and I just sat there. I sat there, notebook-less, wiping away mascara stains on my cheeks, in old stretched out maternity pants, a hooded sweatshirt – braless. I had my phone, but I was only using it to send my husband death texts: "I f*ing hate you, I'm so done."

To which he responded, "Have fun wherever you are."

My name was called after the fourth comic. I ripped the mic out of the stand and started ranting – completely unhinged. About work, psychological torture, misogynistic colleagues, exhaustion and feeling like a stranger in my own body. And I got laughs. A lot of laughs. *Why were they laughing? I wasn't even trying to be funny.* No one had any idea who I was. I wasn't a comedian, I was just some lady that showed up at midnight with a very real life on the brink of a complete nervous breakdown. *And I killed.*

In the cab home, it felt exhilarated. I felt like I finally found what I am supposed to do with my life. I'm supposed to be a stand-up comedian. Finally my childhood showbiz dreams were resurfacing.

I called Marla the next day and told her, while I enjoy voiceovers, I'm going to give stand-up a try. She kvelled and oooh'd and ahh'd and told me, "Call me when you're on a big stage – and stop by for a coffee every once in a while. Love ya Bubby."

I also told Paul that I'd found "my thing." He was his normal British self: Supportive, slightly smug and said, "Ok, lovely."

Since that night, I've been on stage at least six times a week for the last six years….

If I don't do it, I'll regret it

A man is not old until regrets take the place of dreams.
— John Barrymore

I didn't set out to talk about this area of my life in any great detail, but then it occurred to me, *why wouldn't I talk about this?* After all, amongst other things — lots of other things — I am a working comedian. And even the most meticulously planned career can surprise you.

If I was sitting at my favorite Manhattan haunt, Bemelmans inside The Carlyle Hotel with Little Elyse, telling her the story of how her life will twist and turn, she would likely cry from deep pangs of stress and pain, but she would also marvel in the spirited relentlessness that she'd find within herself. She'd probably also be amazed that Bemelmans *does* let kids in the (very) early evening hours. If I told her that at 32 with a failing marriage, two tiny children, a biological clock occasionally whispering, "diapers seem appetizing again" I'd develop into a stand-up comedian; I think she'd cripple with exhaustion. For one thing, just writing it is exhausting me, Big Elyse. But more because she'd understand us flawed humans fantasize about the perfect time, with the ideal circumstance, to act on any sort of initiative. And this one? Becoming a comedian? Getting on stage to tell jokes in a room full of strangers? This requires a special brand of inexplicable lunacy.

Rule # 33: There is Never a Right Time

What are you waiting for? You'll sleep when you're dead.

I approached comedy like a structure-obsessed business executive. Why? Well, because I was accidentally, *and it really was an accident*, brought up in the corporate world, where 1+1=2. We read journals, attend peer groups, schedule meetings in allotted windows of time, pretty much work like cogs in a wheel. So, my approach to comedy was the same: disciplined and scientific.

True, I did start making sand footprints towards the comedy sea without realizing it: The voice overs, acting classes, improvisation classes and teams and my *piece de resistance*, my midnight desperate escape where I vented it all out. But going up on a stage in front of a mic for one night didn't make me a stand-up comedian, it made me more of a curious schmegegge. I needed to devise a plan, a master blueprint for how I was going to implant myself into the real stand-up comedy scene.

I began to use my resources at the improv theater. They offered a pretty rudimentary stand-up comedy class, which I took. Twice. What can I say, I'm an avid learner but a slow one. I do my best learning 1:1 and my teacher recognized that, a guy by the name of Chris Griggs. He was nice enough to help me write jokes outside the classroom. We'd sit in a WeWork space I had for an hour a week and he'd literally show me how to write a joke, what was funny about it and why. Noticing my complete ineptitude to "find the funny", or *his version of funny*, he'd regularly stop the session and say, "Why do you want to do this again? You already have a job – a great one. Do you know how difficult it is to make money in stand up comedy?"

I'd rattle off a million reasons but I couldn't quite find a way to articulate: *I had a calling.*

After those short-lived stand-up classes were over, I came across Manhattan Comedy School, run by a producer who works with new talent at Gotham Comedy Club in Manhattan. I didn't know if the school was any good, but they had aggressive SEO skills and were affiliated with a well-known club. Check sent and off I went. There I had a wonderful teacher, Ross Bennett, who was an older, talented comic who never quite got to the comedy level he wanted to, so he spent his golden years teaching new comics the art of writing a joke, structure, cutting the fat and, of course, performing all of our scratch masterpieces. Ross's class met once a week at night and after the first couple of classes, he told his students where to find open mics. It turned out there were more than one, *and none of them were in attics at midnight*. These were rooms inside comedy clubs and bars, held during the day, where comics go to practice and test out their material.

I had no idea how I was going to swing this considering my full-time position, but I knew I had to get to these open mics if I was going to give this (even a hobby) a try. I found a daily 3pm open mic at a Hawaiian-themed dive bar in Alphabet City aka, the lower east side, called Otto's Shrunken Head. The bar had a dark, dingy room in the back with a stage and a microphone that looked like it could use a good polishing.

But 3pm? *Ugh*.

I remembered a little piece of advice my uncle who was a retired bigwig over at Fidelity once told me, he said: "A good manager values their employees. He/She understands everyone works differently and as long as an employee gets their work done and their numbers are up, I don't care where they are – as long as they are delivering." I didn't work for him, but not only did I change my own management style in my 9-5, I took his advice as if he were my own boss and upped my game.

I began waking up at 6am, kissing my babies goodbye to be in front of my computer working at 7:30am. At 11am, I'd eat lunch (always at my desk to maximize time efficiency), and by 2:30p, I left for the mic and would return to my computer by 4:30p. I never skipped a meeting, never slacked. I'd just leave my office, jump on the subway, scramble over to Otto's, pay $5, patiently wait amongst the other comics for my 5 minutes of stage time, work on my bits and then dash back to work.

I did this everyday.

I would take Ross's class three times. It was worth it because I could see my scheduled writing time and disciplined open mic attendance was paying off. I was *just barely* getting the gist of stand-up comedy fundamentals. A lot of this was simple exposure and experimentation. Like a teenage girl and her heartthrob crush, I had so many crushes on stand-up comedians. And I couldn't believe how easy they made this seem. I just couldn't get over the level of work that goes into this. But that's how any of the greats are, right? They make it look like a slice of pie.

Some of my favorites, most influential (but not limited to): Totie Field, Joan Rivers, Joy Behar, Judy Gold, Susie Essman, Don Rickles, Woody Allen, Mario Cantone, Ray Romano, Chris Rock, Marion Grodin, Gilbert Godfried, Chris DeStefano, Adam Ferrara, Lisa Lampinelli, Larry David, Seinfeld, Jim Gaffigan, Paul Reiser, Roseann Barr, Robin Williams, Bernie Mac, Richard Lewis, Leslie Jones. One of my all-time modern favorites? Sebastian Maniscalo makes me laugh so hard that I could swear I'm having an anaphylactic seizure. I'm choking. I can't breathe. I go home very happy.

And these days, some of my favorites to watch are the *comic's comic*, which special brand of comedian that kinda makes a wink to us other comics. Colin Quinn, Dave Attell, Jessy Kirson, Bill Burr, come to mind here. I adore watching comics work. Since my dive into stand-up, I would go to the clubs and watch all the live shows that I could. Now, six years in and I don't even laugh anymore. Not because I'm a misanthrope, not usually, but because most comedians *don't* laugh. For me, when I'm watching stand-up, I'm studying what's happening on stage and thinking: *Wow that was funny or that was savvy crowd work or that was hack - or, do we really need to hear another d*ck or p*ssy joke?* My favorite thought while watching comedy is: *Wow - they're original, they're special, they're going to make it.*

So, going back to when I started. Over time, I learned from fellow open mic'rs (what newbie comics are called), where *other* open mics were, who was producing shows and much to my surprise, I started to get booked inside little indie rooms (read: a comedy show with anywhere from two to ten people in the audience).

I remember the first time I saw my name printed on a comedy flier. Immediately, *and totally sanely*, I began to fantasize about my future. First comes the comedy show flier, next the closing on my Park Avenue penthouse. And, in a couple months, I'll fly private to Hollywood for a walk-through on the set of my talk show. Maybe I'll ask the driver to swing by Doheny Drive, see if any homes are on the market; or better yet, maybe I'd prefer a water view and stick with a bungalow in Malibu, one on the pacific side of the PCH, where the balcony looks out onto sea, of course with a dry beach underneath the deck. *Ding dong, Barbra Dahling, can I borrow a cup of sugar?*

Oh my god, Ma' call your mahjong friends, I'm on a flier. I made it. With a lot of time, little sleep, grit, learning joke structures, styles and overall comedy writing, I had put together a measly five minute act.

ONE FATEFUL DAY at Otto's, I learned the famed comedy club on the Upper East Side of Manhattan, Comic Strip Live, would be holding auditions for the owner, Ritchie Tieken. Ritchie, a comedy legend, who sadly passed during the pandemic, was not only known for owning the world-famous comic strip, but his biggest credit was discovering and managing a young Eddie Murphy. The guys at the mic — and I was always the only girl there — told me the audition process and I admit, it was pretty grueling. We waited in a line that wrapped around the city block to receive a ripped piece of paper with the date of your audition on it. You'd arrive at the club and perform your five minutes in front of Ritchie. My piece of paper had a spot time of 11pm, when the room was filled with drunks, lovers, both or nobody. Luckily my date was in only two months time, so I didn't have to stew and let my neurotic brain get the better part of me.

When the date arrived for my 11pm audition, I arrived at 9pm. I did my time and afterwards Ritchie called me over and the conversation went something like this:

"How long have you been doing comedy?"

"Three years."

"Really? Three years?"

"Maybe two and a half."

"Do you make money?"

"Yes. Well no. Well, I'm an executive on Wall Street so I make salaried money, but in comedy? Maybe five bucks someone tossed me after a bar show. So, no, I don't make any money in comedy."

"You're special."

"I'm married."

"No. You're different. You remind me of a combination of a young Joan Rivers and a young Fran Drescher. One day, you're going to be a star. Let me work with you. You've passed. Congratulations."

"What's passed?"

"You can now work late nights here at The Comic Strip. This can be your home club."

That was how it went. I couldn't believe it. Actual stage time.

I was so excited, I showed up at the club the next afternoon and bought a couple of t-shirts they sold behind the bar (the ones the wait staff wear); I was elated. Just because you've "passed" didn't really mean you were performing regularly. I'd get about two late nights spots a week, which were anywhere from 10:30p - 12 am – on weekdays. This was not easy with a 9-5 career and two small children at home. I was exhausted.

My time at The Comic Strip was magical anyway. I loved watching the pro comics work on stage. Refine their bits, work the crowds, how they can garner swaths of laughter in unison. One of my favorite moments was getting to watch Leslie Jones work out her Netflix special at the club. She would drop in four times a week in leggings, a baggy t-shirt, sneaks, a brow-sweat towel and with every performance she was more memorizing. After she got off stage, I remember her being so hard on herself. One late night, I caught her walking out the door and said: "Wow, you were great tonight," and introduced myself.

To which she replied, "Thanks. It was fine. I missed one word."

One word? I thought.

And that's when I really realized I was in the world of words, which is particularly endearing for me because as a younger girl, I had a love of language (and large) collection of thesauri. But that moment with Leslie was also one of my first times realizing how much pressure comedians put on themselves. I admired her fierce work ethic; I love her and her comedic style to this day.

I also had some not-so-pleasurable memories these days, like the time one of my Comic Strip comedian friends told me about an NBC audition opportunity. Yes, the television station – *and do we still call them television stations these days?* NBC was scouting up-and-coming comedic talent for their NBC Diversity arm. By the time I found out about it, I had already missed the New York auditions, but the next one was going to be held in Nashville, Tennessee at Zanies Comedy Club. Eager beaver that I am, I quickly cashed in my airline points, flew to Nashville and slept on the street in line with other comedians waiting for the limited-space-first-come-first-serve auditions. Now naturally I didn't "sleep" because I thought murder would pounce upon us at any moment, but I was laying quasi-horizontally in filthy clothes, I was cold yet ambitious. And yes, I do remember worrying, *am I having a temporary lapse of sanity: Harvard… Wharton… two gorgeous babies… and there's Mommy, four states south, 'sleeping' on a concrete sidewalk waiting for* a chance.

While I was working at The Strip, I also started doing the new talent shows at Gotham Comedy Club. Gotham was much larger than the Strip and at any given moment on their amateur shows, big – *no huge*, names in comedy would drop into the club to work out new material. I've seen Jerry and Gaffigan more times than I can count. And it's nothing but completely bewitching.

My "other" life continued… on a non-comedy note: Around this time, I ended up getting divorced, but I'm intentionally leaving it out of the book because it was very painful. Unfortunately once I lost my job at GFP, I guess I did have a temporary lapse of sanity, because I suffered a major nervous breakdown. My darling, dashing gem of a husband Paul who was on my side for so many years, *and really the one person who supported my creative endeavors – without question –* was gone. It was my fault and it wasn't entirely my fault. *I mean, you know how that goes, right?* Marriage is hard. And he was no angel. Like any human, he had his issues and I had mine, but for the sake of our two gorgeous daughters (and because this isn't a memoir), I'll save the divorce details for another time.

What I can say is now, as I write this, we only live three blocks apart, we co-parent our little dolls together and I'd literally be six-feet under without him. He's part of my lifeblood and I love him dearly.

Rule # 34: Take Care of Your Life

For marriage and life, don't let anything get in the way of your mental health. No job, no work trip, no deal - nothing is more important than your mental health and your family.

BACK TO COMEDY, my savior. To be a good comic you have to be comfortable with being bad. Not knowing if they are laughing *with* you or *at* you. Lucky for me, I had so much training on the latter. And I did it all, and still do: Open mics, ballsy audition opportunities, amateur shows, indie shows, real shows, out of town shows. *Every single day...*

... until the dreaded pandemic. When that happened, the clubs and stages were shuttered which is not ideal for a comedian who, at the time, was only four years in. Comedians started performing in parks, in bus lanes, on Zoom and then a small sect of us, *ahem moi*, also turned to podcasting and social media. On social media, particularly TikTok, we could talk to the world, try bits, vent – anything for the stage outlet. All of my family, friends, and probably strangers, didn't know if I was actually a comedian or a schizophrenic, but fortune favors the bold, or the insane. Maybe I touched a nerve, found an audience, got lucky or just some algorithm just smiled on me, but my TikTok and Instagram took off and I was able to amass something in the number of 165,000+ fans online. My podcast, *New York Tawk with Elyse DeLucci*, which has had 90,000 downloads, is a weekly conversation I put out into the oversaturated podcast universe on motherhood, my ex-husband, my crazy Italian family, comedy, dating, food, money, divorce, shopping. Sometimes I get stopped in the street, *or on the supermarket deli line*, but I'm not interested in podcasting and social media stardom. I'm a real, live stage comedian and that's the art form I love. *Though, I will say yes to a talk show and animation voice-overs thank you very much.*

While the pandemic was raging, I spent a lot of time digging out of that vacant stage time. I still do a minimum six mics a week *plus* any and all stage time.

I'm having success and I'm also paying my dues. I don't take any stage time for granted. It's obsessive, it's grueling, it's exhausting but exhilarating.

Rule #35: Obsession Can Be a Good Thing

This rule came not from my family, but from a CEO friend who said: "Elyse, to be great at something, is to be obsessed. Obsession for the job, the process, improvements, it's powerful. Wanting it isn't enough, it's about wanting and being obsessed by improving it.

I'm thankful that some veteran (Italian) comics scooped me up and brought me on stage with them: Bret Ernst had me out in Vegas opening for him. Mike Marino took me to various clubs and theaters, and as of late, Vic DiBitetto has graciously invited me to tour with him as his opening act. Being on the road, which is completely different from a New York City club comic, allowed me to develop new comedy muscles. Through the amalgamation of all of the things I've done from shows to social to podcast to the road, I've finally found my comedic voice.

That changed everything because *I was already funny*, I just had to be myself on stage. I'd been using comedy to cope with anxiety and pain my entire life! For all the learning and classes and coaching I had, you just can't learn personality. What can I say? I got a knack for words, I'm a natural showgirl, a natural schmoozer. I spent so many years in business hiding as an undercover Italian that it feels good to finally be me.

So find your voice, be yourself, have fun, work hard. I wish that I could tell you that's the formula and if you follow it you're golden. As I said at the beginning of this book, life isn't that easy, or predictable. The truth is that showbiz, like the mob or Patagonia vested corporate America, is business.

So...

Rule # 36: Go Where the Work Is

Where else would you go?

As a comedian , if you truly want to get good, develop, you come to the comedy mecca, and work in Manhattan. But know that being at the center of things is no guarantee, the competition is stiff. I'd bet my sad 401K out of the eight million people that come in and out of Manhattan daily, four million of them are trying to become comedians. Stage time is everything and it is extremely competitive. Don't get scared by the competition, though, in the words of Frank Sinatra, "If you can make it here you can make it anywhere."

For that matter, so is the almost-mandatory talking through the screen via social media. And face the trolls. Oh, you have to ignore the noise, because like in any industry, there are people that are negative and want to steal your thunder. What I learned in the corporate world, and it is entirely the same here, the good ones, the ones who've broken through, made it, aren't threatened; they're supportive and encouraging. For me, I'm focused on the work, the writing, and the originality. Because that's one thing you cannot take away.

The comedy community is marvelous. Like every other group from high school to Wall Street, comedy definitely has its hazing period for newcomers. Nothing says "parties over" when the new mom in old maternity clothes shows up at the open mic. On the other hand, it's also like joining another "family." Yes, there are rules, and there is competition and rivalries, but it is mostly a strange family or tribe that is hard to understand unless you are part of it. There's nothing like it. No matter where you're located, comedians experience the same struggles, wins, frustrations, and together we speak in a shared language. Many of us, outcasts, misfits in our own right, and have a love of sharing our view of the world. One of the beauties about comedians is we can look at the same picture and all find something different to say about it. And we do it neurotically, vividly and sometimes poetically.

Truth be told: I met smarter people in comedy than I did on Wall Street and at school(s), the best comics are brilliant, razor sharp, quixotic thinkers.

A Few Words on Mental Health

I think the saddest people always try their hardest to make people happy because they know what it's like to feel absolutely worthless, and they don't want anyone else to feel like that.
— Robin Williams

I think I might be nuts. Not necessarily the kind from Barbra Streisand's 1987 film, *Nuts*. Surely you remember that film, right? ...Her mother and step-father deem her mentally incompetent to avoid a public scandal, which lands Barbra's character, call girl Claudia Draper, in a psych ward unless she can stand trial to prove herself sane. *If you haven't seen the movie - you must - it's terrific. I love you, Barbra!*

I've haven't visited the psych ward *yet*, but sometimes I do have gladiator battles inside my brain. By self-diagnosis, I have PTSD, general anxiety disorder, a touch of OCD and a splash of depresh. *Charming, right?* I mean, you're reading what I'm writing, what did you think, I'm coming out unscathed? And what my mother's probably thinking as she's reading this, in the words of Cher from Moonstruck: "Snap out of it!"

I live my life in a lot of pain from my past. We all do. There was that 'sticking out' childhood and adolescent years, to which I know so many of us can relate. There is my family:

I don't hear happy stories of my childhood (or any stories for that matter), I don't see old photos or home movies, though I know they exist *somewhere*. I think that it's been overshadowed by the unorthodox and violent way in which my parents got divorced: From my father's sharp exit, stage left and all the restraining orders my mother had on him. What can I say? I have abandonment issues: Emotional from my mother and physical from my father. *Thanks guys.*

I felt, and feel, a lot of shame. Carry that kind of baggage from your childhood and there is no way it won't have a profound effect on a marriage. Children, those wonderful, beautiful gifts have a way of bringing out the best in people. Particularly after our first daughter, Annalise, was born, traditionally emotionally reserved Paul began showing, *vague glimpses*, of unconditional love not only to baby Annalise but to me too. The truth is that I didn't know how to handle it. I wasn't shown enough love, I didn't have enough self-love to accept love from others. So, I pushed Pauly the Tooth away. It was all very dizzying and still is: When I was young, I was an independent wildflower and when I got married, I morphed into a codependent.

Though, I found a way to survive. And I'm not going to lie, drugs helped. *Drugs prescribed by a real doctor people. We've been over this.* But how I really coped with my life and life's 'adventures', was by using them to motivate me. I can't tell you why I was motivated by adversity. Maybe my fight or flight response kicked in? If I had to guess, I think I was so overwhelmed and drowning in the deep end, that swimming was my only option.

My therapist, Dr. Long has had a profound effect on me. To my close friends, I would refer to him as my "paid-for parent." He helped me cope. Anytime I'd ruminate on topics, anxiously recap stories or just sulk, he would give *his rules*: "Ignore them" and "People remain themselves." If I told him a sad story, he would cry. And usually on his own, because even in my most private sessions, I was holding back my emotions.

He taught me that being sensitive is okay and being vulnerable is healthy. He encouraged me to buy my Manhattan apartment (because he knew it would please me and The Tooth, as opposed, to say, pleasing my family). He encouraged me to take risks, to keep going.

And, when I unfairly lost a corporate job I adored, he made me realize that I've measured my successes and filled the voids with my professional work. *Which is not okay*. Sure, it is natural to be proud of your work and professional achievements, but that can't be your entire self. For one thing, as Dr. Long *repeatedly* taught me, work and success doesn't absolve me of the pain. He made me exercise (which I loathe), and continue to nurture and love myself on the inside. The truth is that *nothing* on the outside will cure me – or any of us. Sorry.

So, I'm not perfect. I'm not splendid. I'm just trying to do a decent job combating my demons for me, my daughters, my future and my craft, stand-up comedy.

For the record, I wasn't even going to put this chapter in here, I went back and forth about it. Then I remembered the words of one of my favorite movie characters, Auntie Mame: "Life is a banquet and most poor suckers are starving to death!"

I think we all have our fair share of mental struggles and starvations, you are not alone. Join me in the banquet of life!

The Best Job I Ever Had

It takes many stepping stones, you know, for a man to rise. None can do it unaided.
— Joe Bonanno

In order to make my Catholic confirmation, CCD (religion class) told my mother I had to complete a volunteer program. What it boiled down to was that I had to get a job, at the age of 13, with no pay. By then, I was babysitting for money so the thought of working for free was horrifying. My mother drove me to a nursing home, spoke to the resident manager and within one week I was their new volunteer "employee" with my name on the schedule posted on the kitchen cork board. It was official, I had my first 'out of the house' job.

And it was utterly depressing. From the outside, it was a nondescript, unsexy rectangle shaped mid-century red brick ranch building on a main road. Inside it had beige and white checkerboard linoleum flooring, a big activity room, a dining hall, an auditorium and then hallways where the residents lived in one-room hospital-style bedrooms. It had a very distinct smell, a mix of chlorine bleach and mothballs.

My job was to show up and do whatever was asked; from cleaning up after snack time, wiping down the tables, walking the residents back to their room, etc. These were their "golden years" and they were basically living in an off-campus hospital. This was their home and these folks were either disabled, completely alone, batshit crazy or a combo of all three. Whatever the case, what all of them had in common was that they could only function in assisted living and this was the place that they were able to afford.

The nursing home had a lifeless feel to it; I guess that's because some residents had family occasionally visit, but many of them never had a single visitor. Everyone's existence was just to exist and ride out the days of their life in what felt like a sectioned off cream-colored school gymnasium. I was there, basically, to keep them company and act as a built-in grandkid. It was pretty boring, very depressing. To be honest, I think my mother derived pleasure from me working this job, because it showed me another type of life. Which I can respect as now I'm a mother myself.

But, I found enjoyable moments; my favorite thing to do was to host afternoon bingo and polishing all the old ladies' nails. There was this one old lady I was particularly fond of, Barbara. She was about 85 years old, couldn't walk and was relegated to this white wheel chair with a big plastic tray top - like a little tykes car for grandmas. I would polish her nails. *"PINK! PINK IS PRETTY!"* she'd squeal. She'd also scream out the most random bingo numbers in the middle of the day, *"N150!"* when there was no game of bingo going on. She had a wacky, child-like innocence about her. Barbra had a mental condition, I don't know what, but she'd whiz around in her white plastic car screaming for her cat, Kitty. "Where's Kitty? Kitty, come to mommy!" And when she wasn't screaming for Kitty, she was calling for her husband, Mort, who died years before.

It was unclear to me if Barbra had kids, but no one ever came to visit. All I knew was that pink was her favorite color, she loved the beauty parlor and she was very lonely. Some days I would come to work and Barbra would be sitting in her big white chair in the corner of the activity room just blanking out into space with a glazed, empty stare. I'd walk over to her and ask her how she's doing and she wouldn't answer. An aid would tell me, "Just leave her, she'll be back to her old self in a little bit." And she usually did, but one day, she didn't go back to her old self. When I brought over the nail polish and began to polish her nails, she spoke, "I never had a job. My husband took care of me."

"Ok."

"Is this your job? It's good to have something to do."

"Yeah, well this is something I need to do for church."

"I miss him, you know. I had a boyfriend down the hall from me, but he died. He wasn't like my Mort because... Wait. Mort's here too. When we're done, can we go find him?"

I was polishing her pinky nail, "I don't know where to look, but I can ask the front desk."

"Oh you're silly. He's probably in our bedroom, reading, waiting for me to come to bed."

Rule #37: Always Help Others

Without this one, the rest of the rules won't really matter. It taught me that a little kindness, even something as small as ten minutes of your time, can go a long way and be impactful in ways you can't imagine. This job paid me more than any job I've had to date.

Conclusion:
A Sign-off From Love Bunny Cottage

So, there you have it. These are the rules I learned growing up and have helped me out in my journey. Hopefully you can use them too, find them entertaining and if not – throw out the book, what do I care?

Now, I gotta run because my dolls are sleeping, the babysitter just arrived and Mommy has to run-out and get on stage. I gotta keep on getting on that stage, because one thing I know is practice makes perfect and we make our own destiny.

So, here's to Hollywood, Baby. If there is a take-away here, it's that there are rules to the game of life, and when you screw them up, remember that laughter is the best medicine.

If you don't believe me, remember the words of the great Steve Martin, "Be so good they can't ignore you."

Xox, Elyse

GLOSSARY

We're family now, right? Well, here's some New York words for you. Some I've used in the book. And some, well, you should know. A little Italian, American, a little Yiddish and a lot of New York Tawk.

Administration, the: The top-level "management" of an organized crime family.

A La Famiglia: *"To the family"*, used as a toast.

Associate: One who works with, but hasn't been asked to take the vow of Omertà.

Awdah: Order, in Brooklynese.

Awfice: Office, in Brooklynese.

Baws: Boss, New York pronunciation of.

Babushka: A scarf around a woman's head.

Bashert: One's beloved

Books: Books are open, books are closed. Promotions, money, and the like...

Boss: The head of the family who runs the show. Aka The Don. Aka Da Capo.
Bridge & Tunnel: New Yorkers from any borough outside of Manhattan.
Bubbe: Term of endearment for a child.
Bum: Useless person. Not a homeless person.
Bupkis: Nothing. Nada. Zilch.
Buttinsky: A nosy person, a meddler.
Capisce: Pronounced, ca-peesh – Italian for 'understand.'
Capo: The family member who leads a crew; short for *caporegime*.
C*apo di tutti capi*: The boss of all bosses.
Chutzpah: Nerve, audacity, the gall.
City, the: What real New Yorkers call Manhattan.
Commission, the: Leading Mafia members to decide on important questions concerning the actions of, and settling disputes, within the Mafia.
Connected guy: An associate.
Consigliere: The family adviser who is always consulted before decisions are made.
Cop: Steal.
Dem Bums: An affectionate nickname for the (former) Brooklyn Dodgers.
Dere: Old New York pronunciation of 'there', ie: 'over there.'
Dey: Old New York pronunciation of 'they.'

Disgraziat': Disgrace.
Doity: Old New York pronunciation of 'dirty.'
Don: the head of the family; see boss.
Dreck: Cheap, junk, worthless.
Drop Dead: Get lost, go away.
Earner: A member who brings in much money for the family.
Eat alone: To keep for oneself; to be greedy.
Fakakta: Ridiculous.
Fanabula: Go to hell.
Fawk: Fork, in Brooklynese.
Five-o: Cops.
Fuggedaboutit: Forget about it. Did I really need to tell you that?
Foist: First, Old New York pronunciation of.
Fongool: Go f*** yourself.
Fugazi: Fake.
G: A grand; a thousand dollars; also see large.
Garbage Business: Euphemism for organized crime.
Gavone: Someone who eats a lot.
Godfather, The: Head of the Mafia family.
Golden Age: The days before RICO.
Goomah: A mistress.
Goombah: An associate.
Initiation: Becoming a made man.
Kvell: Feeling happy and/or proud.

Kvetch: Complain.
Kick up: Give a part of the income to the next up in the command chain.
Made Man: An inducted member of the family.
Make bones: To start shit, make trouble.
Mamaluke: A fool.
Mannaggia: God damn it.
Medigan': A non-Italian.
Mensch: A good man; one who does good deeds.
Meshugana: A crazy person.
Mezzamort: Half dead.
Mob, the: A single organized crime family; or all organized crime families together.
Mobbed up: Connected to the mob.
Mobster: One who is in the mob.
Musciad: Mushy or sick.
Naches: Pride and joy.
Noive: Nerve, old New York pronunciation of.
Nosh: Snack.
Oath: Becoming inducted as a made man.
Omertà: To take a vow of silence in the Mafia, punishable by death if not upheld.
Outfit: A clan, or family within the Mafia.
Oobatz: Crazy.
Oy: An exclamation, a cry, an expression.
Paisan: One of us, Italian person.
Paying tribute: Giving the boss a cut of the deal.

Plotz: Collapse, faint.
Points: Percent of income; cut.
Program, the:: The Witness Protection Program.
Rat: Someone who turns informant.
Rat Mother: A despicable person.
RICO: Racketeer Influenced and Corrupt Organizations Act.
Schlemiehl: An unlucky person.
Schlep: To drag.
Schlock: Cheap, shoddily made.
Schmegegge: An idiot, a nonsensical person.
Schmooze: To chat.
Schmutz: Dirt.
Schtupp: Sexy time.
Schvitz: Sweating.
Shiksa: A non-Jewish girl.
Skeevotz: Disgusting.
Stunad: Stupid.
Sculabast': Pasta strainer.
Shakedown: To get money from someone, or maybe just a scare.
Shylock business: The business of loan sharking.
Sitdown: A meeting, esp. with another family.
Soldier: The bottom-level member of an organized crime family who is made.
Strunz: Strong.
Struppiau: Half of a moron.

Spring cleaning: Cleaning up, hiding or getting rid of evidence.
Tax: To take a percentage of someone's earnings.
Tchotchke: An inexpensive trinket.
Tree: Three. Old New York pronunciation.
Ubatz: Crazy.
Uddah: Other. Old New York pronunciation.
Ugatz: Bullshit.
Underboss: The second in command to the boss.
Underworld: Beneath proper society.
Whaddayagonnado: What are you going to do? in Brooklynese.
Waste Management Business: Euphemism for organized crime.
Whack: To murder, put a contract out.
Wise guy: A made man.
Woods, the: What real New Yorkers refer to as a forest or a park.
Wise girl: Elyse DeLucci.

ABOUT THE AUTHOR

Elyse DeLucci is a stand-up comedian and business executive. She's currently the SVP and Chief Digital Officer of a commercial bank and formerly the Head of Digital Revenue & Strategy at one of the world's largest financial exchanges. Elyse received her undergraduate degree from St. John's University and has completed Executive Education programs from Harvard Business School in Digital Strategy and University of Pennsylvania's Wharton School of Business in Managerial Economics and Leadership.

She lives with her two daughters in Manhattan, New York.